SAGE was founded in 1965 by Sara Miller McCune to support the dissemination of usable knowledge by publishing innovative and high-quality research and teaching content. Today, we publish over 900 journals, including those of more than 400 learned societies, more than 800 new books per year, and a growing range of library products including archives, data, case studies, reports, and video. SAGE remains majority-owned by our founder, and after Sara's lifetime will become owned by a charitable trust that secures our continued independence.

Los Angeles | London | New Delhi | Singapore | Washington DC | Melbourne

ATTITUDE IS EVERYTHING

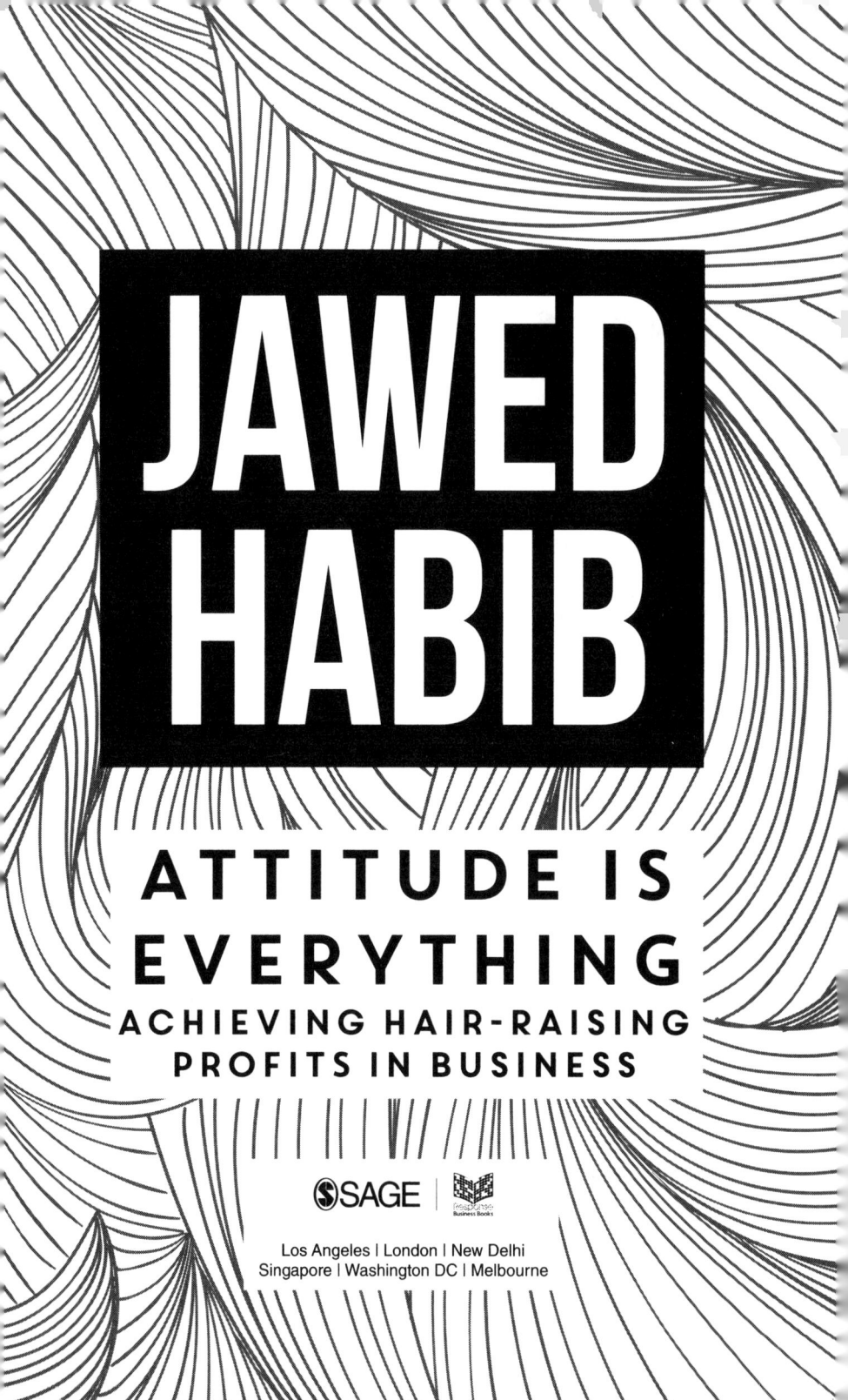

Copyright © Jawed Habib, 2020

All rights reserved. No part of this book may be reproduced or utilized in any form or by any means, electronic or mechanical, including photocopying, recording or by any information storage or retrieval system, without permission in writing from the publisher.

First published in 2020 by

SAGE Publications India Pvt Ltd
B1/I-1 Mohan Cooperative Industrial Area
Mathura Road, New Delhi 110 044, India
www.sagepub.in

SAGE Publications Inc
2455 Teller Road
Thousand Oaks, California 91320, USA

SAGE Publications Ltd
1 Oliver's Yard, 55 City Road
London EC1Y 1SP, United Kingdom

SAGE Publications Asia-Pacific Pte Ltd
18 Cross Street #10-10/11/12
China Square Central
Singapore 048423

Published by Vivek Mehra for SAGE Publications India Pvt Ltd. Typeset in 11.5/15 pt ITC Stone Serif by Fidus Design Pvt. Ltd, Chandigarh.

Library of Congress Cataloging-in-Publication Data Available

ISBN: 978-93-5328-799-3 (PB)

SAGE Team: Neha Pal, Sudeshna Nandy and Rajinder Kaur

Dedicated to every professional who has the zeal and enthusiasm for growth

Thank you for choosing a SAGE product!
If you have any comment, observation or feedback,
I would like to personally hear from you.

Please write to me at **contactceo@sagepub.in**

Vivek Mehra, Managing Director and CEO, SAGE India.

Bulk Sales

SAGE India offers special discounts
for purchase of books in bulk.
We also make available special imprints
and excerpts from our books on demand.

For orders and enquiries, write to us at

Marketing Department
SAGE Publications India Pvt Ltd
B1/I-1, Mohan Cooperative Industrial Area
Mathura Road, Post Bag 7
New Delhi 110044, India

E-mail us at **marketing@sagepub.in**

Subscribe to our mailing list

Write to **marketing@sagepub.in**

This book is also available as an e-book.

CONTENTS

Acknowledgements	ix
Chapter 1: Get Out of Your Comfort Zone	1
Chapter 2: Make Persuasion Your Pay Cheque	25
Chapter 3: Be Unafraid of Experimenting	47
Chapter 4: Old Ways Don't Open New Doors	71
Chapter 5: The *Aam Aadmi* Model of Business	95
Chapter 6: Taking the Leap into Franchising	115
Chapter 7: My Indian Way of Marketing	139
Chapter 8: Going Global	159
Chapter 9: Giving Back to the Society	175
Chapter 10: My Journey and My Learnings	193
About the Author	211

ACKNOWLEDGEMENTS

I, as author of this book, sometimes wonder what led me to write a book on the subject of attitude in business. When I think deeply, I feel that there is a compelling need to address the subject because, at the end of the day, it is all about the game of attitude.

I would like to begin by offering my gratitude to my parents, other members of my family, my team, franchisees, including master franchise and unit franchise, show organizers and every single professional of my field who, in different ways, has shown me the importance of having the right attitude.

I am extremely fortunate for having worked with people who have supported me on my journey, particularly in the formative years of my career. Many of them, through their presence and actions, have guided me in this journey.

I have been lucky to have great friends who have been there in all phases and challenges of my life. These friends have always been honest in their criticism of me and this has helped me grow and be what I am today.

ACKNOWLEDGMENTS

LIFE BEGINS AT THE END OF YOUR COMFORT ZONE.

NEALE DONALD WALSCH

> NOAH BELIEVED THE RAIN WOULD COME; RATHER THAN LISTENING TO OTHERS, HE FOLLOWED HIS HEART AND DID WHAT HE THOUGHT WAS RIGHT. ESSENTIALLY IT IS SAYING DON'T WAIT FOR THE NEED TO ARISE, PLAN AHEAD AND BE PREPARED.

Have you heard about the story of Noah from the Holy Bible? Noah, a shepherd, decided to construct an ark for his family and for himself in preparation for a catastrophic flood. After the ark had been built and Noah and his family had entered that ark, it rained for a period of 40 days and nights, destroying everything in the surroundings. Had Noah not built the ark, he and his family would have had a similar fate like others.

Who doesn't love to be in a comfort zone? That is the reason it is called 'comfort' in the first place. But it is also a place where it is difficult to try anything new. Although you can certainly stay in your zone every once in a while, remember that it is important that you venture out.

> I COULD HAVE EASILY REMAINED IN THE COMFORT ZONE BUILT BY MY GRANDFATHER AND FATHER AS THE COMFORT ZONE IS A BEAUTIFUL PLACE, BUT NOTHING EVER GROWS THERE.

Life is a journey which starts from the mother's womb and then slowly advances through different phases and different stretches. At times, the pace is rapid like the gushing streamlets that run through small hamlets on the mountains, and sometimes it meanders slowly past the cities, towns and plains.

Every journey is an experience, but the experience varies as it varies for individuals. Every individual has a *maqsad* (motto), some realize it early and some later, while some don't realize it at all. Their wishes only remain as unfulfilled dreams because they allow themselves to remain in a zone where they are comfortable and happy.

Although happiness and comfort are apparently not synonymous, still it has been noticed that comfort breeds happiness which then encompasses the 'being' aspect in such a manner that an individual forgets the efforts that he/she had made to achieve that comfort and that state of happiness. The individual remains in that state without realizing that comfort and happiness are temporary. However, with time, the same comfort and happiness that one had longed for and achieved become mundane and suffocating. It is like a mountaineer who strives to reach a peak; once he reaches there, he is so overwhelmed by the beauties of nature that he/she decides to stay back; at nightfall, that same nature turns so harsh that the happiness enjoyed a few hours ago fizzes out. The beauty of the morning is a menace at night. To make that joy everlasting, one will have to push it and shove it into the room called memories, and then get rid of that contentment and put extra effort to descend as there is another peak waiting to be reached. Satisfaction is good, but it does not last forever. So shun it like poison the moment one is satisfied with that satisfaction.

All of us suffer from this deadly satisfaction. It kills the urge to seek, to achieve. Thankfully, it did not happen to me.

I WASN'T BORN WITH A SILVER SPOON

> I WAS BORN IN RASHTRAPATI BHAVAN WHICH IS ONE OF THE MOST BEAUTIFUL BUILDINGS EVER BUILT IN INDIA BY THE FAMOUS BRITISH ARCHITECT, EDWIN LANDSEER LUTYENS.

Like its grandiose structure, its existence looms large over our nation in whatever way one can perceive, be it political or social. My grandfather, Nazir Ahmed, was the official barber of Rashtrapati Bhavan. Our family was from Jalalabad in Uttar Pradesh. In 1936, my grandfather started working in the Viceroy's House. He used to serve the two most powerful men in this country during the pre-Independence days, Lord Mountbatten, the last Viceroy of India, and thereafter Pandit Jawaharlal Nehru, our first prime minister. After my grandfather, my father got this job. It is a hierarchy, a lineage that is passed from one generation to the next for all who worked in Rashtrapati Bhavan. It was then considered an extremely premium job because it came with different sorts of incentives and emoluments such as free quarters, the best of medical care, free education for the children and finally the tag, 'I work and stay in Rashtrapati Bhavan'. Nothing can be more lucrative than this for the citizens of a country like India. Even today, those who are working over there take every possible step to retain that position or ensure that their children enjoy the same 'luxuries'. For them, life starts and ends within this estate of 330 acres.

However, if one thought that we lived in one of the 340 rooms of Mr Lutyens' creation, then it would be wrong. There were separate quarters for the support staff and according to the nature of work, this allotment also varied.

> BARBERS USED TO BE GRADE D OR CLASS IV STAFF ALONG WITH THE *DHOBI* (WASHERMAN), THE CARPENTER, THE PLUMBER AND OTHERS IN THE GRAND RASHTRAPATI BHAVAN.

Our quarter was at the backend of Rashtrapati Bhavan. There used to be a series of 10 feet × 10 feet rooms one after another. Each quarter shared a common wall between them. A quarter was split into three parts. At the front, there was a small drawing room about 3 feet in breadth and 10 feet in width, followed by a 5 feet × 5 feet living-cum-bed room and at the end there was a 2 feet × 10 feet space for cooking. If one wished to call it a kitchen, he may say so, but the same was just enough to set up a *choollah*. There were 10 or 12 such quarters one after another, lined up like blocks to form one series. There were similar such series of quarters for the Group D employees. There were common toilets for the inhabitants of these quarters. We never had the 'luxury' of our own toilet. In the front of these series of quarters, there was a huge open space and a *peepul* tree (*Ficus religiosa*) which used to be the socializing zone for all of us.

I still have some vague memories of my life in Rashtrapati Bhavan. I remember my first school was there. It was a primary school. I do not distinctly remember its name, but I can reminisce going to that school. My father had several friends who were our neighbours too. I might have had friends too, but I do not remember their names. For me, that

10 feet × 10 feet existence in the sprawling Rashtrapati Bhavan was the root of my life. I will always stay connected to that, but that did not stop me from branching out into the world. The most important and also threatening aspect of that existence was its security. Life was smooth, safe and comfortable. And this sort of existence, I feel, is the quicksand of life. It will suck you into such depths from where you will never emerge. That existence's apparent safety and security become an unbearable heavy armour around you, a situation when comfort leaves and frustration grasps. Life no longer remains secure because one has stopped growing and started decaying. Nothing can be worse than this. At that point, acceptance and repentance are the only two things left. Thankfully, such a thing did not happen either to me or to my family.

Apart from the incentives we enjoyed during our stay in Rashtrapati Bhavan, which I had just mentioned, there was another significant one. It was our proximity to the Viceroy and then to the Prime Minister. As is rightly said, the barber's mouth is closest to the king's ears, and we were fortunate enough to have a close and intimate relationship with the two creators of today's India. These two gentlemen played a crucial role in the growth and development of our family and business. When Lord Mountbatten was winding up his stay in India, he advised my grandfather to send his son, my father, to England, specifically London, for formal education on hair services. At that time, it was something unheard of, even more so for a family where skills of cutting hair is an act of natural inheritance. None was supposed to think while passing on the skill to his offspring and none doubted while imbibing it. It is like the family wealth, which only changed hands from one generation to another. No one questioned the quality of the education or the efficacy of the skills learnt. It was accepted as the best that they could get from their predecessor to lead a healthy and respectable life. My father, however, realized the importance of the message conveyed by the Viceroy and thus started a new journey for all of us.

In those days, it was not easy for a Group D government staff to travel abroad for vocational education. Apart from the bureaucratic shackles, there were also financial constraints. Whereas the former could be managed through recommendation letters from the top echelons of the government, the latter was more difficult. I heard that my mother had to sell her ornaments to fund my father's education at London's Morris Masterclass. After completing his education, he returned to India but did not go back to Rashtrapati Bhavan. First, he started working in a beauty parlour named Roy and James. In 1971, he joined the Oberois. After 13 years, in 1983, he started his first salon Habibs Hair & Beauty Salon, and two years later, he started Habibs Hair Academy. This was India's first-ever hairdressing institute, which marked the

> I HAVE SEEN MY FATHER MAKE THIS ARDUOUS JOURNEY FROM CYCLING TO WORK IN RASHTRAPATI BHAVAN TO RIDING A BICYCLE TO THE OBEROI HOTEL AND FINALLY BEING CHAUFFEURED TO HIS OFFICE IN HIS JAGUAR, ONLY BECAUSE HE REFUSED TO BE COMPLACENT.

journey travelled by an unknown barber from insignificance but cushioned by a cosy government job to become India's first-known celebrity hairdresser-turned-entrepreneur.

I NEVER WANTED TO BECOME A HAIRDRESSER

I never wanted to be a hairdresser. Strange it may sound, but it is a fact. My other two brothers had already started helping my father in the salon. I too visited it regularly, but hairdressing never attracted me. I wanted to be a hotelier or rather, let's say, I felt attracted to a job in a hotel. It may be because of the acquaintance our family had with the Oberoi family. Mr P. R. S. Oberoi advised me to learn a foreign language as I wished to pursue a career in his industry. So, I started studying French literature at Jawaharlal Nehru University (JNU). It was around this time that I went to London and, on the insistence of my father, I joined his alma mater, Morris Masterclass.

MCDONALDS: FIRST BUSINESS CASE STUDY

While studying in London, like several youngsters, I started working in McDonald's. It is probably the most natural course of action for anyone pursuing a degree in a foreign land, but for me, it turned out to be an extraordinary and exhilarating experience. The part-time job at McDonald's was not just a job but an eye-opener for me. The systems and processes that were followed in McDonald's surprised me. Everything was so meticulous and so well documented that anyone could become an efficient resource in McDonald's. I worked in all the departments and learnt a lot on the job. These two experiences—education in Morris and the work experience at McDonald's—changed my way of looking at life. My eyes opened. In those months, from November 1986 to July 1988, while I got my first lessons in hairdressing, I also got my first business management class on building a process-driven human-resource-centric organization.

> IT STRUCK ME THAT IF MCDONALD'S CAN SELL A BURGER UNIFORMLY ACROSS ALL GEOGRAPHIES, I TOO CAN OFFER HAIRDRESSING SERVICES ALL OVER THE WORLD IN A PARTICULAR PATTERN.

Upon returning to India, I started working in my father's salon. My love for haircutting kept on increasing day by day. I loved working with my clients. I loved talking to them, hearing their stories, their successes and travails. It was around this time that I had a client who used to tell us his stories about travelling to different countries in different airlines and his experiences at different airports. This used to be our favourite topic of discussion while cutting hair. I was young and all these things were new to me. His stories attracted me, fascinated me. I started imagining myself in those flights, airports and countries. The seed of my love for travelling was planted then.

Even now I love travelling. I love visiting new places. I love meeting new people because each meeting is a unique experience, a new learning. Working in the salon helped me understand the mind of the client. While most hairdressers in our country take pride in uttering the names of the rich and the powerful who are their clients, I never felt any attraction towards it.

TREAT YOUR CLIENT LIKE A CELEBRITY, NOT YOURSELF

CELEBRITY HAIR STYLING NEVER FASCINATED ME. INSTEAD, I FELT THAT WHOEVER WALKS INTO MY SALON SHOULD BE TREATED AS A CELEBRITY.

A customer getting the sense of being a celebrity would go back with good memories, and he would come back again to relive those memories. To do that, the first thing that is needed is to start a conversation and build a relationship with the client. This entire activity is so fascinating that I love to do it even now. So, I spend a lot of time in salons, across the length and breadth of India.

The core of personal and business relationships is trust, love and respect. Without these three, there cannot be any relationship, forget business relationships. Here is one such case of a successful relationship. My partners from Kolkata who believed in my dream that a hairdressing school can be successful outside Kolkata are still with me. They have invested their time, money and careers, and they have grown to become an important and integral part of my organization.

Training new professionals was also a part of this exercise of relationship building. When you train people to become skilled professionals, you build a network along with imparting education. With this mindset, I started teaching and sharing the knowledge that I had gained. Most people used to think that hairstyling is an act of artistry, but it is not so. There is a science behind it, and it has to be understood properly to become a good hairdresser.

I loved teaching. In fact, if my first love is hairdressing, my second love is education. The love for these two has taken me to different corners of the country. Whenever I got an opportunity to impart education through seminars and workshops, I never said no. I never thought of my financial gain. It wasn't a priority. I just went, met new people, shared my knowledge, exchanged ideas, learnt their psyche, saw their problems and realized their dreams.

INVEST IN EDUCATION LIKE A VENTURE CAPITALIST

A venture capitalist is an investor who supports small companies and provides capital to start-up ventures that wish to expand. For me, my companies are my students who are aspiring hairdressers. This is what I have been doing for the last 25 years, at least 50 seminars, workshops or masterclasses a month. In the beginning, the seminars were addressed by my father and even by my brothers. Later, I started having my own seminars because I realized that I could create a connect with the students the moment I was on the stage. I made them feel special and connected. Initially, my workshops used to be over seven days, then it came down to three days and now it is mostly for a day. However, the number of participants kept on increasing. From, around 15 to 20, it has gone up to 400 to 500. I have been attending seminars not just in the metros but in several small cities and towns. This travelling and interaction helped me gain huge experience. Today, I can proudly say that I know and understand the thinking and mindset of Indian hairdressers. This particular understanding has played a significant role in the growth of my business.

As I ventured out of the cosiness of my father's salon by way of attending and addressing seminars or by cutting hair in other salons, I realized that there is a tremendous opportunity to grow and spread the business of providing good, hygienic and proper hairstyling to Indians. But it was not an easy job because none at that time thought that uniform hairdressing services can be replicated across salons and then multiplied across cities and states. That was a time when hairdressers were content with two or three salons. They were proud of showing off their celebrity clients' list. They used to work in their salons day and night but hardly taught anyone how to do

Jawed Habib Master Class at Khan Market Salon, New Delhi

the same work efficiently because there was a sense of insecurity—what if my junior becomes better than me. Hence knowledge remained blocked, good practices were not shared and business growth was stifled. All these are signs of an immature and unorganized industry. It had to change and I pioneered.

While I was in my pioneering mode, India was also on its way to economic liberalization, which started in 1991.

Organized retailing by the giants such as Pantaloons, Shoppers Stop and Westside had just started. More and more people were demanding good-quality salon services. Footfall in our salons was on the rise too. A bullish sentiment prevailed everywhere. I was still working along with my father and brothers. Wherever I went, I noticed a positive mood barring a few here and there. I realized that it was time to spread our brand and expand our business. A boom in the Indian retail sector was ensuing and we must grab this opportunity was what I felt. Rather. I can also say that growth in India's retail business would have remained incomplete had the wellness sector not joined it. And to achieve it, one needed money and trained manpower. We had successful salons. With funds and trained hairdressers, we just needed to replicate the model. It was just that simple and it was not just that simple too because we were content with our two, three or four units. Ours were already considered a premium salon. Being located mostly in South Delhi and catering to the who's who of the crème de la crème of India, we

JH Hair Master Class

Mastering the latest professional cut & color techniques is a significant part of a hair stylist's profession. This course is created for the hair stylists of all levels, which will add a completely new confidence and perspective on hair styling. This will give you an all new, innovative approach to the hair dressing world.

Our Professional Team at JH Khan Market will teach you the advance hair styling techniques as per the contemporary trends & technology through this 15 days Hair Master Class.

Course Contains:
- Advance Cutting Techniques
- Advance Coloring Techniques
- Advance Finishing Techniques
- Latest Styling Tools Training
- Professional Styling Products Education
- Professional - Consultation Skills
- Live - In Salon Training

Calender 2018

8th	January - 2018
12th	February - 2018
12th	March - 2018
9th	April - 2018
14th	May - 2018
11th	June - 2018
9th	July - 2018
13th	August - 2018
10th	September - 2018
15th	October - 2018
12th	November - 2018
10th	December - 2018

Course Content:
Practical and Theoretical

Duration:
15 days

Time:
11.00am - 3:00pm
Monday to Friday

11:00am - 5:00pm
Saturday - Sunday

Price:
₹ 45000 + GST

Certificate upon completion of course

44-Khan Market, New Delhi-110003 | jh@jawedhabib.co.in | +91 11 43646809 | Helpline : 9899996699 | © : 9310075347

Jawed Habib 15-Day Master Class held in June at Khan Market Salon, Delhi

were proud to consider ourselves successful. We were comfortable with whatever we were.

Venturing out to newer geographies or partnering with unknown people would have been breaking the shackles of comfort and that was the last thing we wanted to do. But I wanted to grow. At a time when most in our industry were happy with a chain of five or six salons, I was dreaming of 100 salons. I knew it was possible, but to achieve it, I required more training centres which would create trained manpower to run my salons.

It is not a shampoo or a cream or a conditioner—the biggest raw material of a salon is human resource. I wanted more and more trained hairdressers, but no one was teaching hairdressing in our country then, apart from ours in Delhi, and it was not sufficient to generate those numbers.

So I had to venture out of New Delhi, convince people around me and partner with new people. In 2005, I opened my first training centre outside New Delhi, in Kolkata, then Calcutta. We took up a 1,000 square feet space in South Kolkata at a princely rent of ₹1 lakh a month. It was a huge amount then and that too for a hairdressing school. So we created a small salon along with the training centre as a backup plan. The response was so high that within a year, we shifted this academy to a 2,200 square feet space and the first one was converted into a full-fledged salon. This is probably one of the biggest leaps I had taken in my entrepreneurial career. Incidentally, these centres are still functionally strong.

PRECONCEIVED NOTIONS ARE LOCKS ON THE DOORS TO WISDOM

One of the principles for success in my case has been the breaking of preconceived notions. In my business empire, Kolkata holds a special space as it is one of the major contributors to our business. It may sound strange to many business experts that the fulcrum of growth for India's biggest salon chain is located in the east, which was considered to be the slowest among all regions as far as economic growth was concerned.

It all started over here. Even today, as I write, out of the 860 salons we have, nearly 100 are located in West Bengal. It is one of the most prized locations of our organization.

Several other national and international salon chains tried to grab a share of this market but hardly succeeded. Our success in West Bengal, primarily Kolkata, is a perfect case for a business study.

This success happened primarily for two reasons. First, I believed that there was an opportunity outside the established markets of the North and the West. It was that weird sense of mine that worked and pushed me to take the difficult decision of doing something rather than sitting back, contemplating or analysing possibilities.

Had I remained comfortable with whatever I was doing and desisted from venturing out to Kolkata, what would have happened? Perhaps I would have taken a long time to achieve what I have achieved today.

The important thing is that I had the courage to get rid of the comfort. There wasn't any need then. The need was generated after the ball started rolling. It is like the proverbial story of Noah's Ark. Noah believed that the rain would come; rather than listening to others, he followed his heart and did what he thought was right. The second important reason behind this success was believing in my team members' entrepreneurial skills, their commitment and dedication. We supported each other whenever one needed it.

Jawed Habib Store in City Centre, Salt Lake, Kolkata

THE SUCCESSFUL TWO-DIMENSIONAL BUSINESS MODEL

THERE IS A TWO-DIMENSIONAL BUSINESS MODEL WHICH I FOLLOW, AND IT HAS NEVER LET ME DOWN.

This is primarily a two-dimensional business model which I replicated across all geographies. On one hand, I let my instinct or gut or sixth sense, whatever one may call it, to identify opportunities and possibilities, and on the other, I strived to create a team that would believe in those opportunities, share my dream and would have a common goal to successfully explore that opportunity. In the process, we got rid of the two things that I think are impediments to growth—comfort and doubts.

Once this model is in place, success is bound to come. At least, it has happened in my life on several occasions.

SUCCESS, FOR ME, WAS NOT EXCLUSIVELY MINE. IT WAS THE SUCCESS OF THE COLLABORATION, SUCCESS OF THE TEAM.

This helped in pushing limits and breaking boundaries. However, it is not that this formula has always succeeded, but that has not stopped me from trying it again and again. For me, every opportunity is a challenge and every challenge is a chance to break free of whatever comfort I am in. I am like a kid who is always excited, always exuberant. I strongly believe that I am yet to be successful, so I am always in search of new avenues, new openings and new prospects.

I do not consider myself successful, the sense of comfort never grips me. It is elusive in my life. It is good. It keeps me charged, always.

DON'T LOOK BACK

Although a few new ideas of mine reaped huge dividends, many did not. But as I said, I do not look back. There were times when I felt that going back is more beneficial than going ahead. Even then, I desisted from it; I looked forward and searched for new options, and my positive frame of mind always helped me in finding one. Mostly it happened because my instincts told me that there is an opportunity and it can be utilized for generating something more or better than what is currently available. I can sense opportunities for creating value. But sensing an opportunity is just not enough. One has to grab it and then take it forward with hard work and dedication to create some worth. It is not always easy. Apart from the sense of identifying opportunity, you need zeal to pursue it and an urge to put that extra effort to overcome the comfort zone in which you are. This is a constant factor in my life.

This book is not the story of my life. I do not intend to write so here, but I will constantly tell small stories or explain phases of my life which have helped me build this business.

I never went to any business management school, but I have succeeded in creating India's biggest salon chain because I learnt all my management lessons from my own life.

Every event and every day of my life teach me a lesson or two, which helps in formulating and changing my business. I am always open to new ideas. I am a listener. And I only look forward. The word backwards does not exist in my dictionary.

MAKE PERSUASION YOUR PAY CHEQUE

CHAPTER TWO

PERSUASION CAN GO THROUGH OBSTACLES THAT FORCE CANNOT.

YUSUF A. LEINGE

> HAD I CALLED THIS BOOK *WAYS TO GET A BETTER PAY CHEQUE*, YOU WOULD HAVE LAUGHED AND ROLLED ON THE FLOOR. BUT YES, THIS BOOK IS ACTUALLY ABOUT THE SKILLS THAT WILL TAKE YOU FORWARD—ONE SUCH IMPORTANT SKILL IS 'PERSUASION'.

Understanding the relevance of persuasion as a pay cheque at the very beginning of my career, from KFC and McDonald's whose business models I will take you through in this chapter, has been instrumental in my career graph and in defining who I am today.

Who am I and what is my profession? Whenever I have asked this question to myself, I have often faced counter questions such as am I a hairdresser or a businessman. Or is it that I am a hairdresser who runs a business or is it the other way around, that is, a businessman who can dress and cut hair. I was never ever happy with these definitions as I never considered myself a businessman; in most cases, it has been noticed that businessmen hardly germinate ideas; instead, they nurture the tree that has already grown. At most, they build an orchard or a garden out of a tree. I am not undermining their efforts or the results they achieve. It is extremely important to increase the wealth of the nation or generate employment in this country. I only feel that I am not cut out to be a businessman.

If I would have been one, I would have stuck to one or two or maybe a few more swanky and sparkling beauty salons in Delhi. I would have been probably happy working with my father. I would have been only servicing clients. I would have been so much in love with my work that I might not have dreamt of sharing my knowledge with others. I have not trodden that path. I have had a different journey.

MY FAVOURITE LESSONS FROM MCDONALD'S

My Favourite Lesson from McDonald's is *VISION IS THE POWER TO SEE THE UNSEEN.*

The vision of an entrepreneur is extremely important. It is his/her guiding light, mentor, teacher and guru. It is the goal, and once the goal is set, the entrepreneur finds a way to reach it.

Ray Kroc, who had a goal in mind, ultimately found his way to reach it. You may not know who Ray Kroc is, but I'm sure that you've heard about the fast-food chain, McDonald's. Kroc was the person behind McDonald's; he had the vision to turn the franchise system into the most successful fast-food corporation in the world.

In 1954, at the age of 52, Kroc wasn't selling hamburgers, but he was a salesman selling multi-mixers for restaurants. When he first met the McDonald brothers whose burger business was in their nascent stage, he knew that it was a goldmine that he had stumbled upon which he could multiply to thousands of restaurants worldwide. Kroc persuaded and then successfully managed to convince the McDonald brothers to sell their franchise rights to him; this created the next-door restaurant where you get your burger from. The rest, as they say, is history.

I have always said that my greatest learning was during my employment days at McDonald's. It was a fascinating experience. Apparently, making burgers and selling french fries along with a glass of cold drink in a restaurant is no big deal but to do it uniformly across 38,000 stores spread over 120 countries through 2 lakh employees to cater to 6.8 crores of customers every day is quite a daunting task. For that, one needs immaculate systems and processes which can be followed by people of different cultures and creed across the world. While it mesmerized me, it also made me feel that a similar mechanism could be created to build the world's largest chain of hair and beauty salons. This was the spark, or rather the flame that has been burning within me since then. It is like the flare stack in an oilfield. It burns in me day and night, month after month, year after year. This is the flame that created an entrepreneur out of me and made me a person with the audacity to dream, and as our respected President Dr A.P.J. Abdul Kalam had said that dream never allowed me to sleep.

It is this vision that gives the entrepreneur the ability to see what others cannot see. It gives him the temerity to perceive what others cannot conceive. Merriam Webster defines vision as the power to see, but I feel, here, for an entrepreneur, vision is the power to see the unseen. This particular ability makes an entrepreneur different from a businessman. He creates new avenues, opens new paths and builds new paradigms, which not just changes the world but creates a new world. Starting from the Wright Brothers to Mark Zuckerberg, there are innumerable stories of individuals building new realms which used to be undreamt and unimagined. But once created, it became so manageable, so believable and so sustainable that everyone accepted it. That is the significance of the vision of the entrepreneur.

BE AN ENTREPRENEUR, NOT A BUSINESSMAN

Yes, I am not a businessman. I am an entrepreneur with the vision of giving a haircut to every citizen of my country. Around this vision of mine, I constantly have new ideas coming up, which help me realize my dream.

I have cited the example of the Wright Brothers and Mark Zuckerberg; there is, however, a distinct difference between the two. Whereas the Wright Brothers were inventors, Mark Zuckerberg was an entrepreneur. They had several things in common. Both of them had new ideas because of their revolutionary thinking and they strongly believed in their ideas. To top it, they had unflinching zeal and unbelievable commitment to their belief. No doubt that these aspects pushed them towards achieving their goal and subsequently success. But there is one distinct difference between the two; whereas an inventor pursues a tangible item or product just for the sake of creation or invention, an entrepreneur adds a business perspective to his concepts. On 17 December 1903, when the Wright Brothers successfully piloted their first aeroplane, they never thought of building an industry out of it nor had they realized that the first flight of human being will create a US $4 billion industry in a century's time. But Mark Zuckerberg knew what he was creating. He knew he was building a virtual society of new citizens, the netizens, who would communicate, interact and transact with each other. He knew that a new world of business would be opening up with his idea.

There is another significant difference between an inventor and an entrepreneur. Although an inventor pursues his/her goal religiously, he/she may not need people to accept it and believe in it. He/she can single-handedly run after it. He/she may fail but his/her zeal makes him/her rise and pursue it again. It is a solo effort. There are several stories where inventors have been chastised by society, rebuked by peers and reprimanded by the government, but they never gave up. Some did not even get recognition during their lifetime. With posterity came all the acclamations and accolades. They died receiving brickbats as bouquets were not in their destiny. Even then, they chased their beliefs. The life of an entrepreneur is different. For him/her to materialise his/her concept, he/she needs at least another person or entity to do the transaction. And for that, he/she will have to convince the other to transact with him/her. Here convincing the other is the key. The person at the other end of the transaction should also have the faith and trust in the entrepreneur's ideas. Otherwise it will not work.

As I mentioned the importance of McDonald's in my life, I will cite the evolution of this organization to explain the point I am making. Dick and Mac McDonald together started their first restaurant way back in 1948 with their 15 cents hamburgers.

> IN 1955, A BUSINESSMAN NAMED RAY KROC JOINED THE COMPANY AS A FRANCHISE AGENT AND LATER PURCHASED THE BRAND FROM THE TWO BROTHERS. EVEN BEFORE THEY MET RAY KROC, THEY HAD 20 FRANCHISE CENTRES AND 8 OWNED OUTLETS. MAYBE THE STORY OF MCDONALD'S WOULD HAVE TAKEN A DIFFERENT TURN HAD KROC NOT MET THEM TO SELL MULTI-MIXER MACHINES TO MAKE MILKSHAKES.

Who is the core entrepreneur in this case? Is it the brother duo who innovated a fast-food eatery or the entrepreneur Kroc who had seen a successful business model within that eating joint? Let the debate continue but what is important and relevant here is that either Ray Kroc or Dick and Mac McDonald believed that there was a successful business model which could be replicated to increase profits manifold. They persuaded the other into believing it and that is the moot point of this leading global food-service retailer.

Let us further study this McDonald's story. Kroc could become the franchising agent of the brothers because the earlier agent had passed away. It is a fact that the two brothers had experienced the franchising model before they met Ray Kroc. Hence, we can also say that the brothers convinced Ray Kroc about the success of their franchising. Or, it can also be said that Ray Kroc convinced the entire world about the success of McDonald's to build this huge chain. Either way, the core aspect is persuading someone.

After McDonald's, if we look into the story of KFC, we will find a similar feature. After the end of the Second World War, Colonel Harland Sanders at the age of 55 tried to sell the franchisee of his restaurant and the secret recipe of his chicken dish. His proposal and recipe were rejected 1,009 times before it was accepted by anyone. Even then it wasn't a smooth ride. After several failures and disasters, Sanders managed to make it big after he sold it to a group of investors in 1964. Today there are 21,000 KFC outlets in over 130 countries. Here too, Sanders succeeded to persuade someone, the 1010th time.

I mentioned these two companies as these are phenomenal success stories which have inspired millions and will continue to do so. No doubt, overwhelming zeal and determined efforts are the hallmarks of both these true stories. But there is another common feature and that is the way the entrepreneurs succeeded in selling their ideas. They prospered because they managed to persuade people to buy their concepts.

SANDERS OR MCDONALD OR KROC DID NOT SELL A RECIPE; THEY SOLD A THOUGHT, A NOTION TO BUILD A RESTAURANT BUSINESS WHICH HAD NOT BEEN EXPERIENCED BEFORE.

Persuasion skill is the biggest skill of an entrepreneur. No matter how great one's idea is, it will not work until you succeed in persuading someone to accept it. Some experts are of the opinion that this skill is more significant than that of leadership, accountability, being focused or having sound communications skills. I do not wish to elaborate further on the level of importance being given to the above skills, but one thing I have always believed is that if an idea is floated with passion and honesty, many can be persuaded. But for that, an entrepreneur has to be confident of his/her concept.

> **I STRONGLY FEEL THAT IF I DO NOT HAVE FAITH IN MY CONCEPT, NO MATTER HOW HONEST AND PASSIONATE I AM, IT WILL BE DIFFICULT FOR ME TO CONVINCE SOMEONE ELSE.**

In most cases, it has been found that a true entrepreneur is so engaged with this concept that there is no shortage of belief. Confidence of an entrepreneur may vary against different situations and parameters and with that varies the success strike rate.

However, the first step one should take even before trying to persuade anyone is to hear him out. The more you hear, the more you understand about the needs of the person sitting on the opposite side of the table. Moreover, your attention towards the person will help you earn his/her respect as he/she will realize that you are concerned about him/her. Be curious to know more about the person but do not be unnecessarily inquisitive as it may put him/her off.

Once you have successfully listened to him/her, you are aware of his/her concerns. The person in front is now like an open book, which has been just read. Talk with him/her in an assured tone and not in a well-I-can-help-you-out manner. Do not try to be sympathetic either. Just address his/her concerns genuinely. If you do have an answer to anything particular, say it. Do not camouflage your ignorance under the cover of gibberish talk. It does not stay unnoticed. Be honest in your approach. It helps in persuasion. A question may be asked: Then what makes an entrepreneur persuade? It is a dream. The entrepreneur will have to sell a dream. A dream of a better life. It can be wealth and prosperity. It can be success. It can be fame. It can be a happy life. Every transaction in this world is the selling of one of these. The products or services that are being transacted are actually vehicles which bring any one of them.

So, to persuade a person, try to convince him/her that by accepting the proposal his/her life will change for good. Craft your success story!

Adding value to your concept is important, and for that, the narration of a success story is equally important.

It is like the cherry topping on the cream of a cake. Nothing sells more than success. The success story only adds to the credibility of the claims you are making against your concepts. It gives a sense of familiarity to the person whom you are trying to convince. He/she can relate himself/herself to the protagonist of the story. He/she dreams of becoming successful too in that manner.

However, never ever try to push your ideas to an unwilling or reluctant person. It bears no fruit. Share your concept only with the one who is eager to hear. One may start off by showing eagerness, but if he/she remains unresponsive, then do not proceed further. Add value to your concept. Desist from sharing it. If an entrepreneur insists on such a situation, it will tantamount to overselling and will devalue the concept. I am totally against it.

IS THE JUICE WORTH THE SQUEEZE?

Persuading someone to believe your cause is the biggest tool of an entrepreneur. However, one needs to assess whether persuasion is going in the right direction or not. Are you overselling your concept? A better way to avoid overselling a concept is by underselling it. Yes, you read that right! An entrepreneur shares some initial thoughts and tries to gauge the mood and response of the buyer. If it is positive, go ahead a few more steps. If the idea is warmly welcomed, go ahead further but not on full throttle. Hold it back. Allow the enthusiasm to grow to such a level that the person is totally convinced. At that point, hold back your selling effort. It will be noticed that the person is so convinced that he/she will prod the entrepreneur to give him/her a chance. He/she will die to grab the opportunity. His/her mind will be telling him/her that if he/she does not take it, then he/she will miss the bus and someone else will cash on it. Any entrepreneur will die to be in this sort of situation as it puts a stamp of success on his/her persuasion skills. His/her job is done.

Persuasion gives the confidence to grow big and the power to act differently. Without it, an entrepreneur is just an idea box—a seed which does not germinate into a sapling. Even after elaborating so much on the persuasive skills of an entrepreneur, I must add that there can always be newer ways of persuading someone. What I just narrated is my experience. Yours can be different. As every human being is different from another and no matter how much we try to categorize it, there will always be one who will do what we have not tried and have not thought. Such is the life of an entrepreneur who does what no one has fancied ever.

GOING AGAINST THE GRAIN

WHEN EVERYTHING SEEMS TO BE GOING AGAINST YOU, REMEMBER THAT THE AEROPLANE TAKES OFF AGAINST THE WIND, NOT WITH IT.
—HENRY FORD

The time I entered this industry, India was witnessing massive sociological and economical changes. Liberalization had just set in. Markets had opened up. Global players in different sectors were setting their feet. The organized retail industry was just waiting to bloom. Clothing and apparel companies were going gung ho. Players such as Pantaloons, Shoppers Stop and Westside had started opening their stores. Commodities too were getting branded and roadside grocers had started facing competition from the Big Bazaars and Spencers. All these stores were multi-branded and the business models were worked out in such a manner that risk was shared between the manufacturer and the retailer. Bata, the Canadian giant, was probably an exception.

They had footprints all over India even before the economy was liberalized, but their stores used to be owned and operated by them. In today's retail jargon, these were company-owned company-operated stores.

Here I am trying to make two points. First, Indian manufacturers realized that it was high time to relook at their distribution mechanism. The traditional model of appointing wholesalers and distributors would not give them their desired market share because the entire paradigm of the market was changing. Second, the new-age retailers were creating attractive market spaces but were offering new business modules different from the usual. They were demanding higher margins and longer credit periods. The manufacturers were in a spot because the multinational companies (MNCs) were ready to accept the new terms and grab retail spaces. Through this turmoil, new vistas of retailing opened up which created new jobs, made the older players more competitive and generated higher wealth.

Unfortunately, all this was happening in the product retailing sector. Although around this time, India's services sector witnessed phenomenal growth that was primarily because of the boom in the IT sector. The traditional service sector to which I belonged was not witnessing any of these structural changes.

BREAKING THE VICIOUS CYCLE

The traditional service sector was a vicious circle and I was desperate to break it.

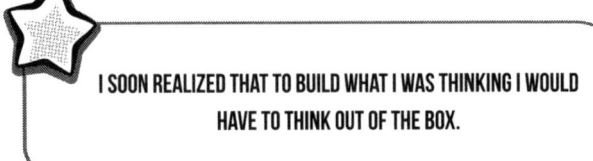

I SOON REALIZED THAT TO BUILD WHAT I WAS THINKING I WOULD HAVE TO THINK OUT OF THE BOX.

I would have to rope in a new generation of entrepreneurs who did not carry the baggage of a brand name with them and who were willing to try something new. But there was a hitch and there were some unanswered questions. Who would build the salon? Under whose name would it operate? Who would bear the operational expenses? How would the profits be shared? And then the most crucial one: Who would bear the losses?

Barber shops and beauty parlours were getting modernized and salons were being created. However, these were primarily on the look-and-feel front as the interiors were only changing because business was growing. Liberalization had, by then, started creating disposable incomes and people were becoming more conscious about their looks and more fashionable.

Nothing was happening apart from this. In fact, none believed that the hair and beauty industry could be expanded in a manner the rest of the retail industry was growing. However, I had different ideas. I was dreaming of building a chain of salons. At that time, I was operating only out of New Delhi, but I had my eyes on the fast upcoming cities such as Kolkata, Hyderabad, Ahmedabad and Bangalore, apart from Mumbai. Expansion even within my city of Delhi was not easy. The sole reason behind it was that none was willing to believe that the salon industry could be expanded through partnerships.

There were many reasons behind this inability to think differently. One was that the industry was highly unorganized at that time. There was no real big regional player, forget anyone operating at the national level. At most an owner had two, three or four salons. Second, the industry was largely driven by individuals. Salons were owned and operated primarily by technicians. He may be either a hairdresser or a beautician or a make-up artist. Although these remarkable group of people were highly qualified, I still had some doubts about their business acumen. They were too possessive about their names, and this possessiveness verged on the brink of insecurity. Hence, on the one hand, they were not ready to share their names and goodwill with other entrepreneurs and, on the other, they never believed that a pan-India expansion was possible.

POSSIBILITIES INCREASE PARTNERSHIPS

I realized that if I could persuade someone to join hands with me, I would also have to answer these questions. I did not have an immediate solution, but I knew that if I could share a portion of the risk involved in the whole venture and operate in a transparent manner, I would be able to convince them. So, I suggested that whoever was partnering with me should just build the salon and then hand that over to me. The salon would run under my brand name and all operational expenses would be mine. This created a positive impact. The potential partners realized that their risk would be limited and they would not have to worry about working capital from the first day. That was a huge relief for them as their total exposure for the venture got reduced. Moreover, they were relieved of any spending on advertisements and promotions because they were using my brand name.

Jawed Addressing a Public Forum in Delhi

As far as my interests were concerned, the primary aim of expanding the chain was achieved. With a common management team, overhead expenses were minimal. By that time, I had already established myself as the leading hairdresser of the country. I had my Guinness record of the most number of haircuts in a day. I had also been appointed the brand ambassador of a leading multinational product company. That gave me extra exposure in the media and added further intangible value to my salons and partners. Thankfully, it worked out to be a win-win formula. Several successful partnerships flourished in cities such as Kolkata, Hyderabad and Ahmedabad. It was around this period that we had an interesting tripartite arrangement with Shoppers Stop, which provided us with space; another partner invested in the furniture and I ran the salons. At one point in time, all Shoppers Stop stores in India had a salon of mine. With that Shoppers Stop offered a different shopping experience to its customers which none of its competitors was able to, and my brand also grew with the exposure. It was an ideal situation for all three of us.

> THE CRUX OF THIS SUCCESS STORY IS NOT SHARING THE RISK BY TWO OR THREE ENTERPRISES BUT IN PERSUADING THE OTHER TWO THAT BY JOINING HANDS WITH ME AND INVESTING IN MY CONCEPT THEIR RISK OF LOSS WAS LOW AND CHANCES OF MAKING PROFIT WERE HIGH.

It was not easy because there were several who did not agree to. Some felt that I was only trying to expand my brand name at the cost of their capital. They thought that a hairdresser would not be able to manage so many salons. They were apprehensive that their investments would go down the drain. Luckily, the number of these people was far less than those who believed me.

My individual success as a hairdresser worked as a catalyst but only up to a certain level. As I was travelling the length and breadth of the country, I met new people every day. They were attracted to me and my work. It helped me find people who were willing to join hands, but to persuade them to invest with me was always difficult. Here, the risk-sharing factor worked well. It made my partners realize that I was also putting my name, fame and money at risk. That really convinced them.

And then we had the success stories coming up from one city after another. More and more people got easily convinced and that helped me in snowballing the partnership model, and soon we had around 100 salons under one brand name. But that was not the end of the persuasion activity. My salon business had reached a crucial juncture before exploding into a manifold network of salons. Maybe, it was the same time for me as when Kroc and the McDonalds started working together.

Here, I decided to change the business model from partnerships to franchisees and another round of persuasion activity started. From convincing someone to become a master franchisee or a franchisee from a partner, I had to make them believe that I was not deserting them; rather, I was just changing the rules of the game. The primary aim of making money by sharing certain values and practices remained the same. I had to persuade that I was taking a bigger risk by sharing my brand name, whose value had grown to an unbelievable level by then. The moment I convinced them about my risk threats, the task of selling a franchisee became easy. They realized that they were partnering with someone who was equally vulnerable and hence neither could afford a failure.

This is another important feature of persuasion. Make the person on the opposite side of the table understand that the business model you are offering is either a win-win formula for both or lose-lose for either. It is not a win-lose model. It helps in establishing your conviction towards your model. Never ever say that the model has only a win-win option. It cannot be so. I do not believe any business model can be so. Hence, be honest and be specific. Sell a realistic dream and never aim for the moon. The moon will remain where it is; only your business will fail. Persuade someone to believe you. If you succeed in doing that, they will also believe in your business model. Success comes with conviction and conviction comes if there is honesty. Without honesty, you will not be able to convince yourself in the first place, leave alone persuade someone else.

If you are honest in your belief, it will automatically get expressed in your words and action. You do not always need excel sheets and powerpoint presentations to prove your point. I have never used a laptop or a computer to do my business. I have only used scissors and have always shared my dreams with conviction and honesty. Believe me, it works miracles.

I have succeeded in persuading people with only these two instruments. Even today, I strongly believe that to expand my network from 850 salons to 8,500 salons or even more, these are the only two things I would ever need.

IN A WORLD THAT IS CHANGING REALLY QUICKLY, THE ONLY STRATEGY THAT IS GUARANTEED TO FAIL IS NOT TAKING RISKS.

MARK ZUCKERBERG

From the first steps of a toddler to the first flapping of wings of a bird, life is all about putting that extra effort in trying to do something new and something different which till then one has not done. It is this extra push that makes an individual do what he/she felt he/she could do but has not done yet. This extra effort has been given different names by different people, but I always feel that this is what separates a winner from a loser. And for that, one will have to get rid of only one particular thing and it is called fear.

FEAR IS A DEADLY INGREDIENT WE ARE ALL BORN WITH. IT KEEPS US AWAY FROM TRYING. IT KEEPS US AWAY FROM ACHIEVING.

If we do not try, we do not achieve. Vice versa, once we fail to achieve, we do not try. It is a vicious circle and in its centre lies fear. Fear can assume different forms and varies with age, experience and environment, but in reality, one is afraid of failure. We fear because we do not know what is going to happen next. It is, therefore, the fear of an unknown situation that prevents us from doing what we wish to do. That is the crux of fear. It proves that fear is a state of mind. Hence, when one succeeds in controlling the mind, he/she can overcome fear. And when someone manages to overcome fear, he/she will try to do new things and with that. one succeeds to reach new destinations and meet new targets.

Get rid of fear and be unafraid to try something new every day. If this can be the mantra of a person, he/she will surely end up doing something remarkable in life. I do not wish to sound philosophical, but over the years and through my experiences in life I have realized that had I not tried to do something new, I might not have done anything in my life. Maybe I would have remained just a barber and would not have become a hairdresser. I would have continued as just an owner of a beauty parlour and not the head of around 1,000 salons. I would have remained just a good hairdresser and not a technician-turned-entrepreneur.

DON'T SETTLE FOR THE ORDINARY

I have succeeded in becoming Jawed Habib, the JH brand, because I have been constantly trying to do something new. I have managed to achieve whatever

I have achieved because I have successfully got rid of fear. I am never afraid. I am never scared of the consequences of what I am doing. I try, so I achieve. At times, I try and I fail, but I learn too. When you do not try, you are not just closing your roads to success, but you are also putting an end to your learning opportunities. No human being ever has managed to achieve anything in life without trying or without getting rid of fear. Fear deletes success from your life. Fear breeds negativity. Get rid of it like you would get rid of poison.

I HAVE NEVER BEEN AFRAID TO EXPERIMENT. AS A RESULT, I TRIED AND CAME OUT WITH SEVEN VERTICALS UNDER MY NAME. THESE ARE JH HAIR & BEAUTY, JH HAIRXPRESO, THE JAWED HABIB, JH ACADEMY, JH HAIR STUDIO, JH HAIR YOGA AND JAWED HABIB SPA YOGA.

—JAWED HABIB

JH Hair & Beauty

JH HairXpreso

JH Academy

JH Hair Studio

JH Hair Yoga

Be Unafraid of Experimenting

Jawed Habib Spa Yoga

DON'T FEAR FAILURE

> ONCE YOU HAVE SUCCEEDED IN GETTING RID OF FEAR, YOU ARE UNAFRAID OF TRYING NEW THINGS. YOU ARE UNAFRAID OF EXPERIMENTING. YOU ARE UNAFRAID OF FAILURE.

There are several stories of entrepreneurs failing and then succeeding because they never failed to try something new again. The success of Bill Gates and Microsoft is folklore now, but we should not forget that his first venture as an entrepreneur was into data management; the company was called Traf-O-Data. Paul Allen was his business partner. He tried to sell his concept, but the product failed drastically.

In India, Narayan Murthy, considered the father of the Indian IT industry, had his own share of failures. His first company was Softronics. It failed within 18 months of its incorporation. After that, he worked in Patni Computer Systems for five years before floating Infosys. There are several such failure-to-success stories of entrepreneurs from all across the globe. All of them tried, failed and tried again and again to achieve success, and this they could do because they were not afraid of trying something new. They did not have any fear of experimenting.

Not just the lives of entrepreneurs, every successful individual has had his/her own share of failures. Amitabh Bachchan himself had said that when the entire world was celebrating the beginning of a new century in the year 2000 he was 'celebrating' a disastrous fortune. 'There were no films, no money, no company, a million legal cases against me and the tax authorities had put notice of recovery on my home,' he had said. By that time, his company, Amitabh Bachchan Corporation Ltd had been declared sick. A megastar in his fifties who had such stupendous success and fan following was in tatters. It was around this time that he started experimenting again. He did commercials and then he agreed to anchor *Kaun Banega Crorepati*, the Indian version of the successful British TV show *Who Wants to Be a Millionaire*. And it turned things around. The story of Amitabh Bachchan is known to all. However, I wish to highlight only one aspect. It was Mr Bachchan's ability to remain fearless which helped him to turn things around. Had he not tried himself in television, the world would probably have not known what one needs to do to be a successful television anchor. We would not have seen another facet of this great entertainer and achiever.

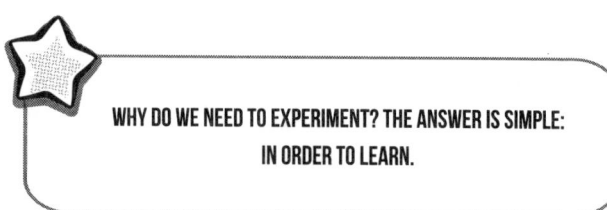

WHY DO WE NEED TO EXPERIMENT? THE ANSWER IS SIMPLE: IN ORDER TO LEARN.

Experimentation helps a person answer the questions he/she is faced with. It helps in differentiating facts from assumptions. By experimenting, one gathers information, which helps in better and faster decision-making. A common mistake that we all generally do is that when we have an idea, we straightaway try implementing it. In most cases, it hits a barrier and we give it up. We conclude that the idea was bad and not implementable. Instead, it should be considered as a trial where we are actually testing the assumptions behind our ideas. Experimentation helps us navigate our ideas through uncertainties and take it to a successful conclusion and is an extremely important part of innovation.

In my journey as an entrepreneur, I have realized that to survive you have to innovate, and to innovate, you have to experiment. The success of an entrepreneur is crucially dependent on his/her innovation skills. Innovation is generally considered as brainstorming sessions, powerpoint presentations and long hours of discussions. I do not subscribe to this idea of innovation. I feel that innovation is the creation of a path through which an entrepreneur will have to take his/her concept under varied sets of parameters to create a new product or a service or a business model. And this journey is full of tests. Rarely does an entrepreneur have a light bulb moment where he/she magically finds an innovative, implementable and scalable business proposition. Experimentation is fundamental to innovation. However, the word has different meanings to different people. Some consider it as exploring opportunities. Some people think of it as finding new ways based on feedbacks of existing products, processes or systems. In a worst-case scenario, it means nothing. In the name of experimentation, the actions undertaken are hollow and meaningless and so they do not generate the expected results. The experiment reaches a dead end. That is certainly not what it should be. But in most cases, it has been noticed that the process of innovation through such trials works miracles. So, an entrepreneur or an organization should be ready to experiment. They may face failures, but they should try to innovate and create something new. And in this entire process, the thing that is certainly not needed at all is the fear of failure.

All of us may or may not have read William Shakespeare thoroughly, but we all know his famous lines from *As You Like It*, 'All the world's a stage, and all the men and women merely players.' I do not want to draw an analogy, but I have my own set of words: I feel that the whole world is a huge laboratory where everyone conducts his or her own experiments knowingly or unknowingly in small ways through daily activities. Some of these are purely for the betterment of his/her own self or immediate surroundings like family or friends. (As I said, when a child takes his first step, he/she is experimenting and trying to walk.) Some take baby steps for the improvement of a society or nation and some for the good of humanity. Their success depends on their zeal and efforts. Some are so zealous that they keep on trying and trying without ever achieving anything. Some are just not interested in changing or trying. So, they end up achieving nothing. And there are many who achieve success without even realizing it. There are some who achieve to usher in change, while there are others who create new paths and avenues. And then there are the stalwarts whose achievements change the entire paradigm of the world.

All of us continue to experiment in some way or the other. It is only the intensity of enthusiasm or passion that differs and creates different sets of successes. The factor that controls enthusiasm is the level of fearlessness that one has.

I have two entities within me. One is that of a hairdresser and the other is that of an entrepreneur. Both these entities have been experimenting with different ideas, concepts and products for over two decades. All were certainly not successful. In fact, I have never looked back to measure my success, leave alone count my failures. These two entities are two different identities of mine. Their environments are not similar and their demands are not alike. However, over these years, there has been only one thing in common between the two entities. Both have been experimenting and trying to find new paths and roads because the motivation to create something modern, something fresh and something acceptable was always the same.

Let me first talk about my entrepreneurial entity. At the time when I was thinking of creating a chain of salons, I had no set pattern in front of me. My journey has been full of innovations through experimentations. I tried to understand the parameters of the market, the needs of the customers and the risks of the partners.

I was fully confident that if one salon of mine could function successfully and profitably, then I could replicate it many more times and across geographies, but there were uncertainties, such as who would invest money, from where would I get trained manpower and how would we manage daily operations. With regard to these three, I knew that I would have to achieve the following three. Investment had to be shared with partners so that risks were minimized. To have trained manpower to run my salons, I needed to create hair academies or training schools in geographically significant locations like in other metro cities. And to manage operations, I needed to have a centralized management team. There was the requirement of managers at each centre who would implement the policies of the central team.

ROUGH SEAS MAKE SKILFUL SAILORS

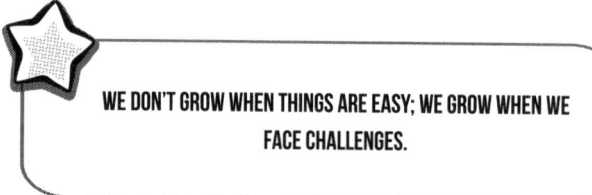

WE DON'T GROW WHEN THINGS ARE EASY; WE GROW WHEN WE FACE CHALLENGES.

The first challenge was to convince a partner to invest in my project. Once that was overcome, then there was the challenge to train hairdressers in different locations. Till then, we had our training centre only in New Delhi, and those who attended the classes were trained by us directly. It would not be possible with multiple training centres. Way back in 2005, we started the 'Train-the-Trainer' programme. The last challenge of having managers was also solved by hiring local talent and then imbibing them with our systems and processes.

Today, all these things sound so easy, but it was not so at that time. Every step and every arrangement were experiments. Some were successful and others were not. For example, we first started off with salons at other locations in New Delhi itself. We asked our partner to build the salon and hand it over to us. We ran it and shared the revenue based on the top line, net of taxes and not of profit as it would have created unnecessary differences with the partner. But what would be the percentage of sharing was the moot point. Again, another set of experiments and a new set of innovations were needed for this.

KOLKATA STORE: A GAME CHANGER

An interesting and intriguing case happened in Kolkata. We had a young lady in her late twenties who was already working with us as a manager for our salons in Shoppers Stop. It may be noted that we had a tripartite arrangement with the retail giant, which is another case of experimentation. I will elaborate on it too. Now, this manager in Kolkata was efficiently running the show and the Kolkata salons were achieving more success than the rest. She was organizing two-, three- and five-day seminars for me in that city. She was seeing young boys from far-away villages of West Bengal coming to New Delhi for undertaking our hair courses. She realized that there was an opportunity of starting an academy in Kolkata as the boys would no longer have to bear that extra expense of travelling and staying in New Delhi.

We, therefore, proposed to her to follow our existing model, create the infrastructure and hand it over to us. We also decided to make it a salon-cum-academy purely to spread the risk over our two businesses. The challenge, however, was for her to garner funds to build this salon-cum-academy. It is needless to mention here that in retail business, real estate is a big cost proposition, be it buying it out or even taking it on rent. Unfortunately, the lady did not have access to that amount of money. However, at our end, we knew that she was enterprising and efficient. She then roped in a partner who decided to offer the space.

The lady was supposed to build the infrastructure of the salon-cum-academy within that space, and we were to run the operations. We decided to share the revenue in the ratio of 20:10:70. The partner who was providing the space was getting 20 per cent, the lady was supposed to get 10 per cent and the rest was ours as we were taking care of all operational expenses. I wish to emphasize here that apart from our own stores, nowhere were we paying rent for the properties. Here also, the real estate was provided to us.

Accordingly, agreements were finalized, but on the day of signing, the other partner who was providing the space backed out. The entire project was about to fall apart. Now, this lady came back to me and asked whether we were ready to pay the rent which was a princely sum of ₹1 lakh per month for 1,000 square feet of space in south Kolkata. Honestly speaking, I was reluctant because nowhere were we paying for space. She had a different explanation to convince me. She said that she was investing money in building the infrastructure of the proposed salon-cum-academy. If the venture did not work, then we would stop paying rent and close the salon. The landlord would get his space back and I could redeploy the staff in other places. However, as the cost of building the infrastructure was hers, the entire risk was hers too, because if the academy-cum-salon was closed for good, cost retrieval for her was almost impossible. She suggested that she would only take 10 per cent of revenue and as we were providing the space, our share would be 90 per cent. She requested to give it a try for a few months. I felt that she had a point and I was convinced.

This was major experimentation for me. I did not know what would have happened if I had not agreed. But let me tell you what happened when I agreed. Never ever had I any doubt of the capability of this lady as she was one of my most successful managers, but the challenge was whether to change and adopt a new business model. Incidentally, this was also our first training centre outside New Delhi and our first major venture in Kolkata. Prior to that, we had salons under our brand name but our involvement as corporate was minimal and here was a different story, altogether. We were getting larger exposure and hence, a bigger risk. Thankfully, the project was such a huge success that in less than a year we had to shift our academy to a new and bigger location. Now, the academy itself was on a space of 2,200 square feet and the entire 1,000 square feet of the first location was converted into a salon. This was a perfect example of reaping benefits through experimentation and innovation. The fearlessness shown by us helped to create value for so many individuals. Both of us were unafraid to experiment and that was the real reason behind the success. Thereafter our business in Kolkata and surroundings grew in leaps and bounds. At present, we have around 100 salons in West Bengal across all formats and brands. The entire model of partnerships snowballed from this successful venture. This will certainly remain a milestone in the growth and evolution of our brand and organization.

THE SHOPPERS STOP MODEL

Coming back to the Shoppers Stop model, here, the retailer provided space, and there was a partner from Ahmedabad who provided the infrastructure by investing in the salons' furniture and equipment. We took care of all operational expenses. The risk of the venture was shared by the three parties. Shoppers Stop succeeded in providing service sales to its customers apart from products of multiple brands. It also gelled with their aim of giving a different experience to its clients. It may be noted that the salon experience in Shoppers Stop was so successful that another Indian retail giant and a major competitor of Shoppers Stop also started following it by floating their own brand, their own salons within their stores.

However, no business model will be perfect forever. There will be lacunae and shortcomings. What may work perfectly with a particular partner or in a particular geography or with a particular brand may not be successful across all partners, brands and geographies. After the successful launch of the Kolkata model, we replicated it successfully in other locations too. But experimentations kept on happening and we kept on changing the partnership model based on the results of the experiments. All these experimentations made us bolder to try new models and innovate newer business structures. In the process, two things happened simultaneously. First, we kept on learning both from our successes and failures. Second, our business and number of salons kept on increasing. Again, I repeat, all this was possible because we, as an organization, were learning and changing.

NEXT CHALLENGE: SCALING UP OPERATIONS

With the growth in the number of salons, I realized that the next challenge would be in scaling up the operations. Managing 30, 40 or even 50 salons from a small set-up in New Delhi was slowly becoming more and more difficult. But my dream was bigger. At that time, around 2006, I realized that to grow larger I would have to be in the business capital of our country. So, I shifted my corporate office from New Delhi to Mumbai. A proper office with distinct divisions such as finance and accounts, HR, legal and administration, training, marketing and promotion and others were created. Management graduates from the leading B schools of India were hired. A proper structure was created to manage the growing business network of the company.

At this point, we reached another crucial juncture which made me sit back, think and work out newer business models. With the growing number of stores, managing through the partnership model was becoming difficult day by day. Several operational issues were coming up. Not all partners were efficient and successful. It was smooth for the units which were running profitably and were registering growth, but for the others, the situation was different. I also realized that wherever the partners were proactive and inclusive in nature, the salons were functioning smoothly. But there were units where the partners felt that their ownership ended with the creation of the unit after which they were only looking to reap the profits. This was a major learning experience for me. The experimentation that we did with the partnership model made me realize that the involvement of the partner was equally important for a salon's success. Hence, I realized that I would have to formulate a model where the partner would be an equal owner of the store or might even have higher ownership than that of the mother brand, the corporate office. Without that, complete inclusiveness would be difficult to create. This made us change from the partnership model to the franchisee mode of operation.

However, it was easier said than done. I truly believe that success is a baggage and its burden reduces your manoeuvrability. The more you are successful, the less is your agility. By this time, we were already nearing 100 salons and I felt that this was the right time to move to the franchisee model. Meanwhile, franchising had just started in India, but again being a flag-bearer in this industry, I had no model to follow. All successful franchising that was happening in India or had already happened by that time was in the goods sector. Nothing was available in the services industry. There were models that were followed in established economies but copying them would not be easy as India was a developing country and franchising was a new concept. So, on the basis of our learnings from the partnership model, we worked out our franchisee model. In 2009, we completed our shift from the partnership model to the franchisee model. Although the broad parameters of this franchisee mode of operations have remained the same till now, we are still constantly working on this model. We are fine-tuning it and trying to make it more franchisee-friendly so that it works well for the parties.

I would like to add an interesting anecdote over here. When we started with the partnership model, we used to have only a two-page agreement. It was not just elementary but was also scrappy. Even our initial franchisee experiments were only 10–12 pages. Today, it is almost a 60-page legal document, covering all aspects of franchising operations, clearly spelling out the roles and responsibilities of the franchisor and the franchisee, and even categorically mentions the services that can be offered from the salons. These changes are taking place because we are constantly experimenting, innovating and changing from the lessons we are learning. We are not shy of sharing our mistakes and not ashamed of our failure. All these were our learning curves. It is like a journey on road, where you meet new people, have new experiences and reach new destinations every day. As I am writing these words, I know, the entrepreneur in me is thinking of newer ideas which will be more contemporaneous—a model that will work successfully for salons located in all tiers of Indian cities and even the *mofussil* towns. It requires a greater understanding of the market and that will come only through higher innovations and rigorous experimentation even in the harshest market condition.

Even while the entrepreneur within me is constantly striving to create excellence through experimentation and innovation, the hairdresser has not remained idle. As the most successful hairdresser of this country, it is my duty to find newer and more cost-effective ways of caring for one's hair. I am regularly offering solutions to hair problems which are extremely common and faced by most of us. These are innovative methods using regular daily items. I am a firm believer of the fact that one may not get the desired results just by using a highly expensive product of an MNC. In our society, there are several methods practised through ages by our fathers and forefathers, which are extremely effective. Interestingly, these practices vary from one geography to another because of the change in climate. And these innovations were not just restricted to haircare, but similar things were also done in other chemical services on hair.

Being in the fashion industry, it becomes obvious that I will have to improvise and innovate to remain fresh and contemporary. There too is a process of experimentation, because, without it, my work will become stale and mundane. It is a constant demand for this industry. Hence, one would have to build within him/her the culture of experimentation to remain sought after. And being the 'Scissor Man of India', it is my responsibility to make my fellow Indians more fashionable.

What I wish to say is that, had I not experimented with fashion, I would not have attained the success that I have today as a fashion icon, because fashion is only about experimentation and creating something new. If I was afraid of trying out new things, I would not have managed to stay relevant in this fast-changing world of fashion.

This is a continuous process. One just cannot afford to stand still or sit back and contemplate that he is through with this share of experimentation or think that whatever he/she has achieved or created is the ultimate. Even if a portion of this kind of thought enters anyone's mind, then take it from me that it is the beginning of his/her downfall. Throughout the history of human civilization, it has been witnessed that those who are unrelenting in their pursuance of excellence and are in a constant strive to achieve something new have remained leaders in their fields. They will have their share of failures, but ultimately they will be winners. Failure is a part of life and certainly an ingredient for success. Whenever one tries to do something new, in whatever age or span of life he/she is in, he/she may experience failure, of which some are negligible and some monumental. At times, repeated failures make a person pessimistic and depressed. He/she tends to give up as it is the easiest option. My advice is never to give up. If you believe in what you are doing, then carry on despite the failure.

To overcome failure, first remove the fear of failure; you will win half of the battle. There are innumerable real-life stories and there will be even more in future, but to have your story etched in history, do not ever stop trying. Life is vast and there are opportunities galore; just embrace it. Experimentations and innovations are just like picking up shells on the seashore. Look ahead at the blue ocean, and you will realize the immensity of the prospect that lies ahead of you.

> WE KEEP MOVING FORWARD, OPENING NEW DOORS AND DOING NEW THINGS, BECAUSE WE'RE CURIOUS AND CURIOSITY KEEPS LEADING US DOWN NEW PATHS.
>
> — **WALT DISNEY**

Almost 2,500 years back, Heraclitus, a pre-Socratic Greek philosopher, floated his timeless doctrine, 'Change is the only constant thing in life', through his famous words, 'No man ever steps in the same river twice'. This philosophy is universal and ageless. The insight that these few words conveyed has made it relevant even today and will remain so in future. We all know that changes are taking place every day and every moment, but unfortunately, we are not always ready to accept it and face it because we are not willing to change ourselves. We wish to remain comfortable in whatever zone we are with the expectation that we will continue to reap the same fruits as we have been doing.

These words are true for an individual and for an enterprise. If we accept that it is difficult for a human being to realize the changes that are taking place around him/her and then take steps to change himself/herself, then we will also agree that this difficulty gains in dimensions for an enterprise, simply because more lives are involved in it. Making everyone change in a uniform manner is a Herculean task. However, it has to be done, as it is inevitable.

TRANSFORMATION: A REALITY FOR BUSINESSES TODAY

Failure to transform closes doors to success, which is quite evident from some of the well-run companies which flopped owing to their lacking ability to transform.

There are several examples of corporations who have not transformed with the changes happening in the market place. Either they did not read the change or were so confident of their previous successes that they did not bother to change. Hence the inevitable happened; the organizations were ruined forever.

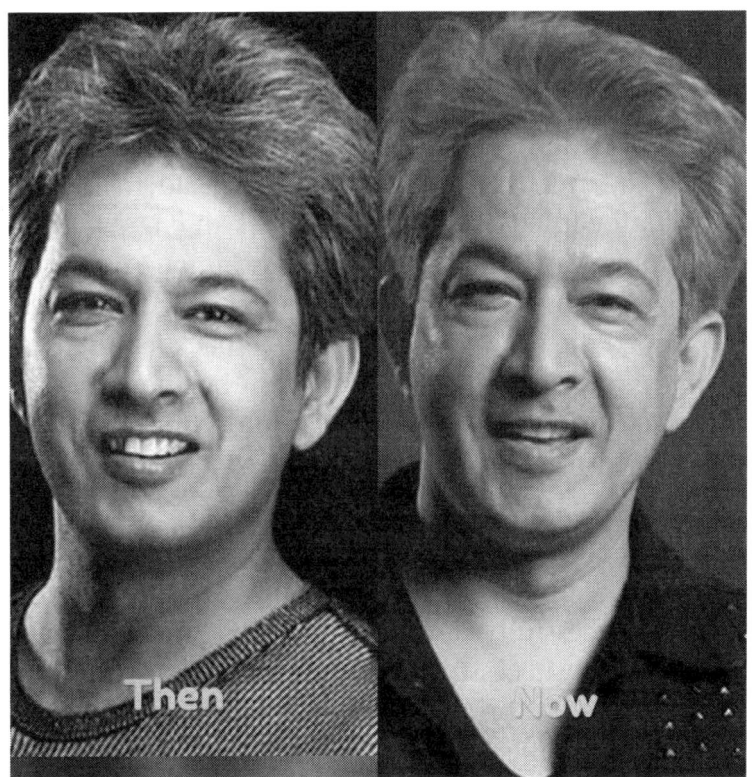

Transformation of Jawed Habib from a Hairdresser (Then) to an Entrepreneur (Now)

TAKING CUES FROM GIANTS

If you ever have a doubt in your mind about some idea or concept, then one of the biggest 'Go-To' is learning from the stories of other businesses. I have followed such examples, which in turn have helped me take a cue and implement it in my business.

Let us take the story of Kodak. It is a technology company that ruled the photographic film market. They were leaders for almost the entire second half of the twentieth century. Then the digital age came. Kodak did not change, and hence it had to file for bankruptcy in 2012. Ironically, it was an engineer and an employee of Kodak Steven J. Sasson, who invented the digital camera and way back in 1975. The company developed the product too but held it back fearing that it might affect its photographic film business. This is a perfect example for a corporation ending up in the pages of history because of its failure to transform.

The story of IBM is just the opposite. In the mid-1980s, IBM was the undisputed leader of the computing world after it successfully developed PC, the personal computer. It was successful because it did not work all by itself. Instead, it brought pieces of hardware and software from smaller players, assembled them and then loaded them with Microsoft Windows. The product became the darling of the market. But this very strategy, which was totally opposite to that of Apple, was the cause for its fall. Soon smaller, smarter and swifter players copied the IBM model. They too did what IBM was doing but in a better and faster way. The giant went into red, and in 1993 registered a huge loss. It had only one option before it. Change the business. So, the leader who pioneered supercomputers gave up its core business of making and selling low-cost PCs and other hardware. Instead, they started focusing on the information technology (IT) services business. Today, it is one of the world's leading service providers in IT. It invested heavily into the server business too. IBM's evolution as an enterprise is being studied regularly in business schools.

Although the above two stories tell two opposite tales, the history of Nokia is unique, as here the two had dovetailed into one. Way back in 1871, a mining engineer Knut Fredrik Idestam commissioned his second paper mill along the river Nokianvirta near the town of Nokia in southern Finland. He named his company Nokia Ab. Around 17 years later, Finnish Rubber Company started producing rubber tyres and goloshes. These two companies and a third company, Finnish Cable Works, came together to create Nokia Corporation in 1912. This new company manufactured colourful rubber boots and it was a huge success. In 1963, the electronic wing of Nokia started producing radios for the army. Within a decade or two, the company made commercial radio and car phones. In the early 1990s, Nokia sold off its initial businesses of rubber and paper and decided to concentrate all its resources on manufacturing cellular phones which could function on the Global System for Mobile Communications (GSM) network. This successful transformation from a traditional paper and rubber manufacturer to a modern cellular phone producer can be best measured by the fact that the company was the highest seller of cellular phones for 14 consecutive years in the world. It started in 1998 and went on till 2012.

But as Heraclitus predicted no man steps into the same river twice, no success is permanent no matter how long it stays with you as the world around changes. With the advent of the Internet, newer mobile companies realized the rising significance of data communication. The age of voice communication was weaning. Nokia failed to grasp it. The company, however, remained focused on cellular phone hardware. Smarter players introduced smartphones. In 2007, Steve Jobs launched iPhone. It changed the entire cellular phone market. Nokia's market share started falling. It wanted to be smart too, and therefore in 2008 it decided to take on Apple with the Android technology, but it was too little and too late. Nokia, the corporate, lost its market share and the brand lost its sheen. Today, it is striving hard to get some recognition in the market which they once dominated and dictated.

The purpose of narrating these stories is to emphasize the fact that success, no matter how big and huge it is, is actually temporary in nature because change is permanent. Corporations and enterprises can accept it when their leaders stop refusing the inevitable. I discussed the journey of only three companies, but there are several who have passed through such phases, successfully or not. Leaders, who have a vision, not only see opportunities, but they can also gauge the forthcoming threats. They know that what is good today might not be so tomorrow. So, they change their outlooks, change their paths and draw new dreams.

EVERY IDEA HAS AN EXPIRY DATE

IDEAS HAVE A SHORT SHELF LIFE. YOU MUST ACT ON THEM BEFORE THE EXPIRATION DATE.
—JOHN C. MAXWELL

Over the years of my entrepreneurial life, I have realized that the way I am doing business is good as long as something positive is happening, and then at times, you face situations when it is not so. These are junctures in life when you sit back and ponder, 'What will happen now because nothing is happening?'

> THIS MOMENT OF 'WHAT WILL HAPPEN IF NOTHING IS HAPPENING' IS THE POINT WHERE ONE HAS TO REALIZE THAT THE EXISTING WAY OF DOING BUSINESS IS BECOMING OLD AND OUTDATED, AND IT WILL NO LONGER GIVE YOU THE RESULTS THAT YOU ARE ASPIRING.

Then is the moment to open new doors. I strongly believe that every idea, like a bottle of medicine, has an expiry date beyond which it is not just stale but poisonous. Unfortunately, such dates are not printed and labelled. It is your instinct that tells you that time has come to think afresh your brilliant ideas, no matter how much success it has brought you.

People often tell me that my business is not susceptible to changes. Why? They think that I am in the business of cutting hair. They tell me that men have been cutting hair for ages and women, breaking away from our traditions, have also started cutting their hair. Their conclusive opinion is that both men and women of India will need a haircut at regular intervals and we are there to provide it. Hence, we are insulated from technological changes and are protected for changing market dynamics. For us, there is nothing new to adapt, except perhaps the fashion factor. Fashion changes and we will only have to change accordingly to incorporate those changes. If we manage to do it properly, we are free of all fears.

BUILDING RELATIONSHIPS: A TRIED AND TESTED FORMULA

BUILD THE RIGHT RELATIONSHIP WITH THE RIGHT PEOPLE AND NURTURE THEM OVER TIME, AND YOU WILL ALWAYS HAVE A LEG UP ON THE COMPETITION.
—PAUL MAY, CEO, BUZZSTREAM

Every idea has an expiry date; however, there are some exceptions to it. The idea of building relationships has been a tried and tested business model for me. At the core, a business organization is nothing but a giant network of relationships. If you fail to build those relationships, your chances of succeeding are not very high.

Our vision is to organize the muddled hair industry prevailing in the country today and hoist it to a level

> GIVING A HAIRCUT IS JUST A PRIMARY SERVICE. I AM IN THE BUSINESS OF BUILDING RELATIONSHIPS WITH INDIVIDUALS THROUGH PARTNERSHIPS AND IMPARTING EDUCATION TO PROFESSIONALS IN THE BEAUTY BUSINESS.

where it equals global standards, and train the aspiring talents and regularly upgrade their skills. We hope to see the practice go global very soon.

BUILDING RELATIONS THROUGH EDUCATION

Let me elaborate it from another perspective. Jawed Habib Hair and Beauty sells beauty services. Education of hairdressers is another important business of ours. Our entire business operates through a network of master franchisees and franchisee. All my customers, partners and franchisees are my stakeholders. I can also say that they all are my customers in some way or the other. For example, if someone invests money in my business, then he/she will wish to have a gainful return; he is akin to a client, who walks into my salon and hopes to get a good service. Hence, it is my responsibility to ensure that an investor or a franchisee or a client is satisfied in the interaction that they have. Then, let us consider the psychology of a student who has just enrolled in my institution. A student is there not just to undertake a hair course, but he/she is actually looking for a profession and settled life once he/she leaves the academy. A student does not want just a certificate but also wants to imbibe a skill in him/her that will help him/her earn bread for the rest of life. So, our responsibility is to make a student a good hairdresser. All these are our touchpoints as an organization where we are constantly challenged by different aspects of our relationships.

In short, there are three sets of people with whom we do business. First, is our students; second, we have the partners or the franchisees and third is the clients. These are three distinct sets of human beings with whom we do business, and like all businesses in this world, here too there are changing market dynamics, unknown and hidden threats, and opportunities galore. Over the years, I have changed my ways of doing business in all these three categories.

Let me take up the case of students or our education business. At present, we have around 65 academies across the country and we are planning to open a few outside India. The first was in New Delhi; we opened the second one in Kolkata and then Hyderabad. The others followed. The numbers are not as important as the journey. For over two decades, I have been meeting students through my seminars, which are conducted all over India. Initially, these used to be five-day affairs, then three- or two-day affairs and now they mostly get over in a day. On this journey, I realized three things. First, there is an acute shortage of education in this industry and people are willing to learn and gain knowledge before starting a professional career. Second, the need for education was hardly realized by the players who have been there in the industry. Third, if I wish to increase the presence of my brand, I need to have more trained hands and that will come by imparting my knowledge to others.

Armed with these three realizations, I started the business of expanding my hair education. The challenge was to reach the maximum number of students in the easiest possible manner and to give them the best education possible so that they can be recruited in the organization for giving the highest quality of service to our clients. Initially, we had our own institution in New Delhi. We were reluctant to share it with others because we were apprehensive that the quality of education might be compromised if it was not directly monitored and overseen by the core team. However, there was the challenge of expanding salons and for that, we needed trained hairdressers.

> I REALIZED THAT THE OLD WAY OF DOING BUSINESS WAS NOT YIELDING RESULTS. SO WE STARTED NEW ACADEMIES IN PARTNERSHIPS AND FINALLY MOVED TO THE FRANCHISEE MODEL.

To ensure the quality of education, the teachers were trained at the central academy at Mumbai through the 'Train-the-Trainer' programme from where they branched out to the centres. The final gradation was also controlled from the head office.

Today despite having 65 training centres in 90 cities across 21 states, we have reached a point where I notice that even this model has limitations. Where do the limitations lie? Today our academies are located in Tier I, II and III cities, but there are many aspiring students beyond these cities who wish to pursue a career in hairdressing. Second, there are many who are working in a different profession but want to become a hairdresser. However, they cannot quit their existing occupations and register for the hair courses. And there is another lot, the uneducated technicians who are mostly employed in the unorganized sectors of our industry. All of them cannot afford to find time or money to undertake a proper hairdressing course in any of our academies. What is the way out? Here again, we are in a situation where existing business practices are unable to find answers for the new problems that we are facing. Hence, the situation demands a change and adaptation to new business opportunities. We realized that the best way of reaching every person is by taking the help of the Internet. Everyone has smartphones and are glued either to YouTube or other channels. We, therefore, decided to launch online hairdressing courses. We thought that they would cover everything from the basics of haircutting to the intricate chemical services.

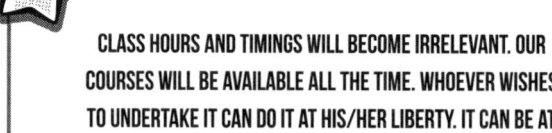

CLASS HOURS AND TIMINGS WILL BECOME IRRELEVANT. OUR COURSES WILL BE AVAILABLE ALL THE TIME. WHOEVER WISHES TO UNDERTAKE IT CAN DO IT AT HIS/HER LIBERTY. IT CAN BE AT THE DEAD OF NIGHT OR EARLY MORNING.

Apart from providing courses, I also conducted one-day hair masterclasses. I strongly believe that this kind of flexibility for students will create a new dimension to skill training in India. Some may call this move thinking out of the box or innovation. Whatever one may call it, I feel it is an effort to change and adapt to new market situations.

BECOMING A LEADING FRANCHISE PLAYER

Now let us take the second business of ours, franchising. This was the perfect example where we realized that the old way of doing business was not generating our expected results. The general concept of expanding business was by to create new sets of infrastructure, follow it up with the hiring of new manpower and then through constant promotion and management control, ensure business growth and profitability.

> THE BIGGEST CHALLENGE IN THE FRANCHISE BUSINESS MODEL IS MONEY. IT IS NOT EASY TO GARNER SUCH BIG AMOUNTS OF FUNDS TO EXPAND BUSINESS IN THAT TRADITIONAL MANNER.

To address the issue of funds, we created the business model of partnerships. It was a unique one at that time, different and innovative. Our business started to expand through these different partnership models. It yielded good results. From a meagre 15–20 salons we moved up to around 100.

Then we faced operational challenges as managing each unit was becoming extremely difficult. Uniformly sustaining the culture of Jawed Habib Hair and Beauty in all the salons and its employees across all geographies was becoming difficult. The then existing model of partnerships was not working. We had two options before us. We could have gone back to the traditional mode of business expansion by doing it all by ourselves or we could opt for the franchising model. We opted for the second. Again, this was an innovative model because till then franchising in the salon industry was unheard of in India. We pioneered it because we realized that the old way would not open new avenues for us.

> IN THIS JOURNEY OF CHANGING BUSINESS PARADIGMS AND CREATING NEW STRUCTURES, I OFTEN FACED SITUATIONS WHERE NOTHING WAS HAPPENING. PATHS THAT HAD BEEN SMOOTH TILL THE DAY BEFORE ALL OF A SUDDEN HAD OBSTACLES ALL OVER. JOBS THAT WERE EASY TO PERFORM SUDDENLY BECAME DIFFICULT. PEOPLE WITH WHOM WE WERE DOING WONDERS UNEXPECTEDLY CHANGED AND STARTED QUESTIONING OUR DECISIONS.

Markets that were responding to our moves, stopped doing so. These were signals which indicated that the time had come to change the track. Entrepreneurs and enterprises should immediately read it, change their course of action and look for newer options. I feel that the instinct and gut feeling of a leader are

Jawed Habib Salon Opening in Maharashtra

extremely important in these situations. They should understand what is good for the organization and then do it accordingly. For that, if changing orbit is necessary, then be it so. In several cases, it has been noticed that an organization saturates all its resources that the existing business structure offers to them. Such situations demand structural changes. I know that it is easier said than done, but that is the only way out.

CUSTOMISING GLOBAL TRENDS FOR CUSTOMERS

Now let us discuss our final set of customers. They are our clients who visit our salons regularly to take service from us. Here too, changing at regular intervals is the only way to stay relevant in this market of fashion. We are constantly looking at the services we are providing.

> WE ARE ALSO SYSTEMATICALLY OBSERVING THE NEW FASHION TRENDS EMERGING IN THE GLOBAL MARKETS. WE ARE STUDYING THESE CHANGES AND THEN INDIANIZING IT TO CATER TO OUR CUSTOMERS.

All that is happening in the global fashion arena cannot be replicated for our Indian clients. Customization is necessary and we are doing it regularly. For example, straightening or rebonding of hair used to be a big-ticket service in our salons, but the interest for this service tapered out. So we introduced smoothening, which involved less harm to hair and also gave a more natural look as against straightening. Although the shine and look of smoothened hair remained for a lesser amount of time compared to straightened hair, still clients opted for it. This service too started losing business after some time. Then we introduced keratin treatment. Like smoothening, in keratin treatment too the hair is shampooed thoroughly to remove dirt, blow dried and then a keratin-based solution is applied. The main difference between these services is that keratin is a naturally occurring protein in our hair and it is replenished during the treatment for healthy, silky hair, whereas in smoothening, we use artificial ingredients which are not always as friendly as keratin.

I have cited the example of only one service. Similar changes are constantly taking place in the salon industry primarily to cater to two needs. First, in meeting the new fashion demands of the clients; and second, by keeping the revenue growth clock ticking. I do not think that there is any other requirement for any salon in this world apart from these two. And to achieve it, we look for new solutions, new concepts and new ideas.

Despite sounding repetitive, I must add, changing from one mode of business to another or discontinuing a successful service is not easy, but one will have to do it to adapt to new situations. I strongly believe that adapting to new situations is the key to survival. It is true both for human beings and enterprises. A single human being can easily change and adapt to new situations, but for an organization it is difficult. However, in this complex and dynamically shifting business atmosphere, need for a change and subsequently adapting to it are extremely relevant. The market is mutable and so are the needs of the stakeholders of an enterprise. Adjusting to it is essential.

And to achieve it, the leader of an organization will have to instil a culture of innovation, change and adaptability within its stakeholders. It has often been noticed that the top leadership identified a faraway threat and then introduced new steps and methods to counter it, but the larger team was not in sync to accept it. To avoid such situations, strategic adaptability is required. Strategic adaptability is a planned ability to react effectively when business and environmental factors change unexpectedly. This is a written definition available in the books, but practising it is not that easy.

Adaptability, as we all know, is the ability to adjust one's outlook or action in response to a change that has occurred in the external environment and over which one has no control. It is a priceless skill for any individual or corporation. There is a concept of strategic adaptability. It applies mostly to enterprises. However, I think that in the current market scenario every individual all over the world should think of himself/herself as an enterprise. It will help him to plan his/her future accordingly.

The biggest challenge with regard to strategic adaptability is that one will have to plan for the unexpected. It is natural that no human being or enterprise can plan or anticipate the changes that will occur in future or the problems and challenges it will face owing to that change. It cannot be achieved no matter what amount of research an organization does or how instinctive a person is. However, a standardized system can be created within an organization, or a method can be put in place whereby one knows how to respond to such changes in those situations. Learning from past experiences is another key capability of an organization. I know that the same situations do not repeat, but the way one reacted earlier should be in one's knowledge. It will help one in not repeating a mistake. At the same time, I must add that recognizing one's mistake is also important. Once it is understood, chances of repetition are low and the capability of adjusting to the new situation is high. A company can continue to increase its capacity to change and adapt to new situations in the same way as it develops new products and services. It is a journey and a continuous process.

TRUST YOUR INSTINCTS

I am an extremely instinctive person and rely highly on my instincts. It is not that by relying on the instincts I am always successful. I have my share of failures too, but I do not ponder over it. I believe whatever decision I had taken at any point of time was the best possible decision that could have been taken.

I may have gone wrong, but on the day the decision was taken, I had full faith and trust in it. I am primarily a man of action. I take quick decisions and go for immediate implementation. I strongly believe that over-thinking and delayed action kill the spirit of the idea. Never ever have I dilly-dallied on my decisions. And I am always open to new ideas. Rarely have I said no to anyone who has an excellent new idea. I give total freedom to the people who work with me. I love to see the result of that work at the earliest. As a result of this nature of mine, I am always knocking on new doors. It means that I always looking for new opportunities. I hardly wait for the existing opportunities to dry up. In my project pipeline, at any point in time, I have several things lined up. Hence, I have never faced a situation where all my existing revenue streams had started drying up because work on something had already started. This approach of mine has always kept me in sync with the existing market conditions. This is also my mantra of adapting to new situations.

TREATING CLIENTS AS BRAND AMBASSADORS

Apart from my instincts, another factor that has helped me a lot to understand changing market situations and their subsequent adaptation is my regular interactions with people from different sections of society. For example, I work in my salons. So I know what my clients want. I am regularly in touch with partners. They share their concerns and problems. They are my eyes and ears. The feedback that I regularly receive from them is extremely important for me to study the changing revenue dynamics of a salon. Then I have my students. The seminars that I address generally have 100–500 students. I learn from them too as they share with me their experiences with their clients and customers. I have been sharing my personal phone number with these students for almost a decade. I have been telling them that whatever problem they face as a hairdresser, they can share with me. I have been addressing their concerns for many years. Then you have social media. I am active on YouTube. My channel has over 5 lakh subscribers. Through all these avenues, I am able to receive feedback. It is important. I take all types of feedback in a positive manner as it gives me an opportunity to improve. It helps me gain more knowledge. These all are my learning experiences. As I said, it helps me adapt to the changing market scenarios. I am always grounded. I know where I stand today and where I wish to go tomorrow, and what I want to achieve; I am always eager to change and I always try out new opportunities.

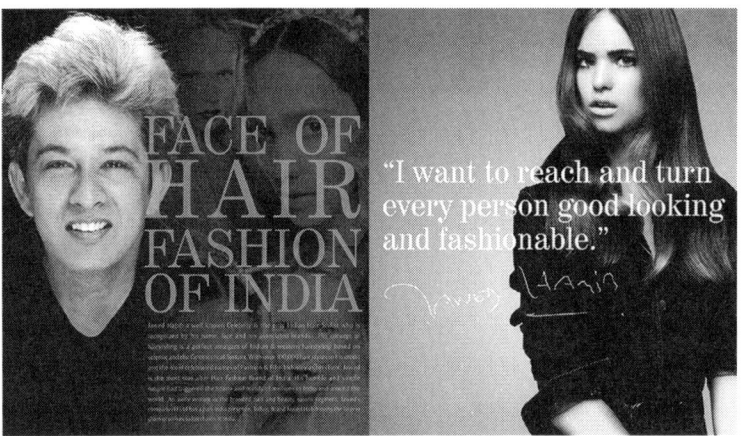

The Brand Cuts Across Classes and Masses

I can do it because I am a very optimistic person. I always see things from the point of how-to-do-it rather than this-is-not-possible. This is why my teams and I are always working on multiple projects, be it big or small. Failure has never bogged me down. In fact, it gives me a boost to put in renewed effort. I do not give up easily and I do not like excuses. If there are genuine reasons for a failure, I accept it and move ahead. My life is like a running train. Every station and every junction gives me new opportunities as new travellers board it. Those who cannot keep pace with me or do not like my ideas or way of functioning are free to disembark. I move on with a new set of relationships and a new bunch of dreams. It has been so till now, and I hope that it remains so in future.

THE *AAM AADMI* MODEL OF BUSINESS

CHAPTER FIVE

CHAMPIONS KEEP PLAYING UNTIL THEY GET IT RIGHT.

BILLIE JEAN KING

THE MASS CUSTOMIZATION MODEL OF BUSINESS

In today's consumer-driven marketplace, it's a smart idea to create custom offerings that meet the specific demands of not just niche customers but of the masses. Several years ago, probably in 2008, I was addressing a small impromptu press conference at Asansol, which is the second-largest and most populated city in West Bengal after Kolkata. I had just inaugurated my first salon in that city. It was a hot sultry day. The salon was located on the third floor of a market building. After the inaugural ceremony, there were the normal congratulations from everyone. My partner was also with me. It was a really happy occasion for all of us. My fans, friends and well-wishers had also gathered. Several people were taking tips from me on hair care and other related things. By that time, I had already established myself as a celebrity hairdresser. I never knew what the term meant, but that was what I have been called. Along with friends and others, several journalists had also come to interview me.

I WAS ONCE ASKED, 'WHO ARE YOUR CELEBRITY CLIENTS?' I REPLIED, 'ANYONE WHO WALKS INTO ANY OF MY SALONS IS A CELEBRITY.'

When I had said these words, I did not know what I had thought or what I was thinking at that point of time but those were the words which encompassed the entire philosophy of my business activity. I am a hairdresser of the masses, and I wish to remain so forever. It is a concerted and determined decision of mine, which I had taken at an early age of my career and it has remained with me.

I keep on telling everyone that I wish to give at least one haircut to every citizen of this country. It appears to be a simple statement of a dream but it means 130 crore haircuts! That is the magnitude of operations I am looking at. This is not a random statement of mine. I firmly believe it, and I wish to achieve it too. All my business decisions are taken to materialize that dream of mine.

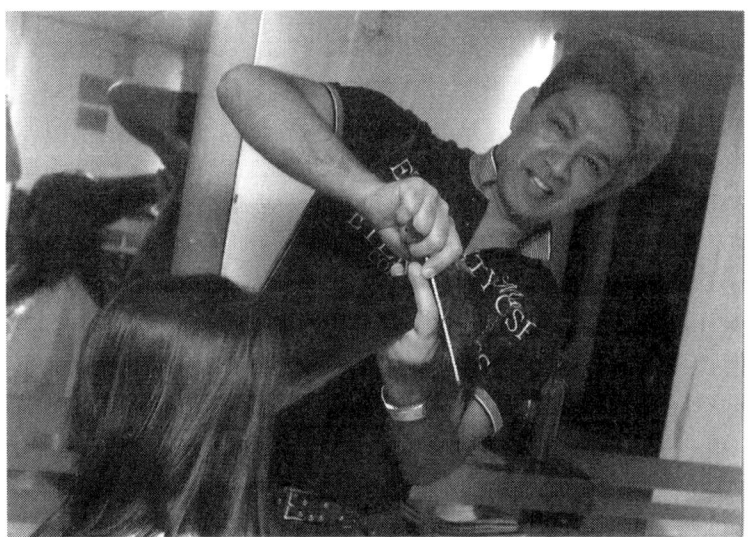

Jawed Working on One of His Clients at His Salon in Khan Market, New Delhi

About 25 years ago, hairdressing in India used to be categorized into two sectors. The first sector was the huge unorganized sector. It was almost 99 per cent of the market. And the rest, 1 per cent or probably even lesser, was where you had the celebrity hairdressers. It is like Mr X is the hairdresser of the following film stars or Mr Y who does the haircut of some famous politicians or cricketers. There was no identity or recognition of the rest of the hairdressers.

On the other hand, in the Indian social milieu, a haircut was considered a mundane activity—a boring thing that men had to experience every month. There was nothing interesting or exciting about it. The sense of happiness or a feel-good factor was never associated with a haircut. Hence, it became a low-end job carried out by a group of professional technicians, who were highly skilled but hardly educated. They were neither well paid nor earned any recognition and respect from society at large. Here is a perfect example where both the service giver and the taker were not happy. People went for a haircut as they had to. They had no option. It was mostly a barber's shop and all these shops were almost the same. Hence, the experience was alike everywhere. The barber who picked up the skill from his father or grandfather hardly had any formal education. He probably never had an opportunity to select this profession. He was just doing what he had been asked to do, and he carried on thereafter. There was no innovation in service offering and no incentive for skill upgradation. In short, it was a dismal situation.

THE BURGEONING INDIAN MIDDLE CLASS

The year 1991 was a watershed year for all Indians. It was probably the most significant year of India after Independence. It was also around this time and in the following years when everyone started taking note of a new segment of the Indian market called 'the Indian middle class'. Its size, purchasing ability and spending power have remained a matter of debate for over two decades now, but what is important is that the sellers of products and services primarily targeted this sector of the market and were rewarded. In fact, it has been noticed that the middle class of any country has played a critical role in driving their respective economies.

This is new-age India. It is not just restricted to Delhi or Mumbai. Even other metros such as Chennai, Hyderabad, Kolkata and Bengaluru came up fast along with cities such as Ahmedabad, Surat, Varanasi, Pune, Jaipur, Kanpur, Lucknow, Nagpur and others. And to succeed in this market, it was important for me to establish and nurture a relationship with the Indian middle class. I always knew that this was the path for me and I stayed on it. This approach of mine has taken me to 24 Indian states. Today I am present in 110 cities of this great country through 864 salons. We service more than 15 lakh customers every year. Even then, I believe that I am only scratching the top layer of the market. By a conservative estimate, if I say that the size of the Indian middle class is 30 crores, then I have reached only a half a per cent of this population. It is still a long way to go.

BUSINESS STRATEGY IN THE EMERGING MARKETS

Coming back to the business strategy I had adopted, let me elaborate it a little more. The primary service that I have been selling is a haircut. It is a job done by the masses and for the masses.

All Indians, barring women and one particular religious community, go for haircuts at regular intervals. As I mentioned earlier, it used to be a boring and uninteresting job. So I tried to bridge these two sections of society with my knowledge, education, systems and processes to bring in the two following features.

The first was training the students and the masses to become hair designers. There were no 10th or 12th-degree criteria, which is the bare minimum requirement for many courses. At an affordable price of ₹50,000, anyone could do this three-month course and get a job of ₹8,000 plus incentives at my salon. For instance, I hire 100 students every year from the remote village of Bongaon near West Bengal and provide them with job opportunities after training them in my hair-designing courses. Education for the masses was my primary business model that could reap great returns from the perspective of profit and employment. This way, these students could earn more respect, recognition and money.

Other than this, another *aam aadmi* (common man) approach was a special treatment to the masses. People would love to come for a haircut, rather than force themselves into it. I introduced programmes such as customer loyalty programmes, which offered a good discount to all customers on their birthdays and anniversaries. I also introduced a service update programme where I would ask my customers about their experience at my store.

HYGIENE FOR ALL

The health of your customers should be of utmost importance to you. Any small or large business unit can only succeed if they keep this aspect as one of the top priorities in their list. For example, in India, there was an age-old practice. Everyone used to go for a bath immediately after a haircut. There was a reason behind it. Getting a haircut was a dirty affair. Unclean scissors, filthy combs, rusty razors and filthy cutting sheets were the primary reason. And on top of it, heat and dust. Hygiene was never considered a significant factor. Hence, a bath was mandatory after a haircut. It also meant that haircut had got nothing to do with fashion. It was just an act of getting rid of unwanted hair on one's head.

We changed it. We made shampooing mandatory before a haircut. We ensured that clean towels and neat cutting sheets are used for every customer. We also made it mandatory that towels and cutting sheets were washed and cleaned after every usage. Hygiene was made the top priority. Our foremost agenda was to make the customer feel good. A good haircut was just a part of it. All these were done to ensure that customer satisfaction was high and that he/she would want to come back again for a haircut. It also meant the end of the practice of a bath after a haircut. He or she could go ahead with his or her daily chores even after a visit to our salon. This was applicable to all our stores throughout the country, even in small towns. I also felt and strongly believed that every customer deserved a good haircut in a clean atmosphere no matter what price he or she was paying. The common notion is that when you are paying a basic minimum price for a haircut, hygiene and cleanliness will be compromised. In such situations, neither the customer demands a clean cutting sheet nor does the hairdresser offer a hygienic ambience. I am strongly against it and I ensured that all my salons, no matter at what price points they were placed, were always clean and hygienic.

On the other hand, we tried to modernize the profession of hairdressing and to do that, I had to bring in education. It was generally perceived that hairdressing was just a skill that could be learnt through vocational training. I agree but, along with the skills, a good hairdresser must learn several other things too. First, he/she should start respecting his/her job and profession. Second, he/she should know how to talk and interact with the clients. Third, he/she should be neat and clean so that people would not hesitate to take a service from him/her. Fourth, he/she must understand the need of the client and then accordingly offer his/her service. Fifth, he/she should have the necessary soft skills so that he/she is acceptable to the customer. Finally, he/she must respect time and money. A client comes to our salon, spends time and pays money for a service. It has to be respected by the hairdresser. All these sensibilities can be incorporated in a hairdresser only through proper training and education. Our training centres impart these pieces of training along with vocational skills.

As you realize, I was consciously managing two large sections of the society at the same time. Both of these groups were equally important for my business model. If one wishes to call it the masses, let that be called so. If one wishes to call it the *aam aadmi*, I will not mind either. The fact that remained constant is that I will have to continue doing it if I wish to expand my business further and reach my dream of giving at least one haircut to every Indian.

PRICING IT RIGHT

For catering to the masses, you need to keep the price in mind, and you have to price it right. The price of a haircut in a Jawed Habib Hair & Beauty salon varies from as low as ₹149 to ₹700. The most premium brand of ours is the Jawed Habib. This is a lounge concept with a cosy unwinding atmosphere. Here the price of a haircut can go up to ₹1,100. These, however, are extremely competitive rates.

Jawed Habib HairXpreso Store, Rainbow Plaza, Rahatani Road, Pimple Saudagar, Pune

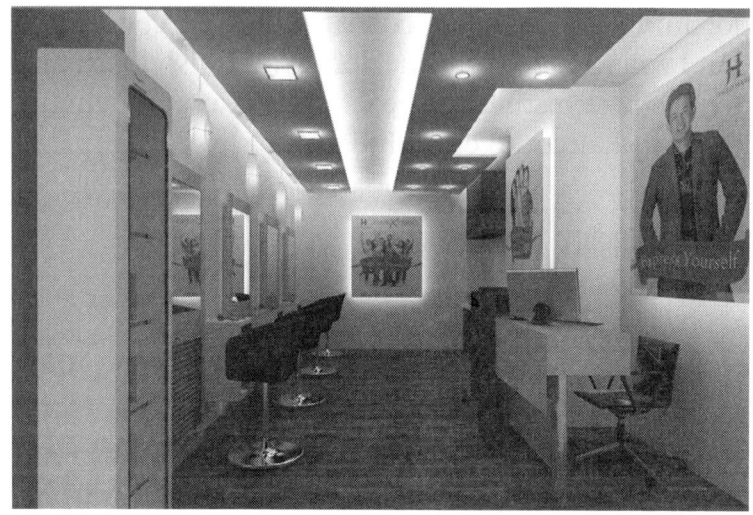

Hygienic Interiors of the HairXpreso Salon

The price of a haircut at a Jawed Habib Hair & Beauty salon also varies with the location of the salon, whether it is located in Tier I, Tier II or Tier III city. Today, we are also present in small *mofussil* towns. Accordingly the price is finalized. The aim is to have as many customers as possible. However, the price variation does not mean that we are compromising on the quality of the service. It is the same everywhere. I am referring to the price of the haircut simply because it generates the highest amount of revenue in our organization, and it is also a primary service that a customer looks for when he/she visits a Jawed Habib Hair & Beauty salon. Prices of other hair and beauty services are consciously kept at par with the market standards so that common people can afford our services. Our aim is to give a good quality service at the most affordable price. And I can vouch that even in this approach, we can generate a healthy bottom line for the corporate (Jawed Habib Hair & Beauty Ltd) and the franchisees to grow. It all boils down to the fact how efficiently we are managing our financial and human resources. It has helped us to beat inflation because we have not changed the price of haircut for several years now.

Another interesting brand of ours is the Jawed Habib HairXpreso where we currently give a haircut at a price of ₹149. This is a unique model of a salon where the price has been kept so competitive that anyone can walk in. JH HairXpreso was launched in 2009. The average size of the salon is 100–150 square feet. These salons are located in high footfall zones. The aim of these salons is to give a quality haircut in the shortest possible time. It is a no-frills approach. Anyone who is in a hurry, can walk in a JH HairXpreso, get a quick haircut and continue on his way. This is the approach.

However, we noticed a strange thing happening. A section of the society which could not afford even paying ₹200 for a haircut started visiting our JH HairXpresosalons. Although my initial thought behind this model was not aimed at catering to this section of the Indian masses, still it happened, and I am happy that it happened.

Let me share a story with you

Sukhdeo, a roadside cobbler, used to work outside just one of our JH HairXpreso salons in Kolkata. All through the day, he was busy mending shoes and chappals sitting on the footpath. Every day he carried his bag full of spare soles, knife, hammer, tack puller, prying tool, thread and needles from his home to this place outside our salon. We hardly noticed him. One day, just before the Durga Puja, which is the biggest festival of this region, we saw Sukhdeo entering our store with three young girls aged between 7 and 14 years. One of our team members went up to him to find out what he wanted. He was expecting that Sukhdeo would be asking for his annual *baksheesh* (tip/bonus). This is a common practice during a festive season in India, and no one minds giving a few hundred to the poor. However, this was not the case. Sukhdeo had brought his three daughters to get a haircut done in our JH HairXpreso salon. Durga Puja was round the corner and he wanted his daughters to look great. All through the year he saw men and women coming and getting their looks changed with just a haircut. He wanted the same for his daughters too. He aspired that his daughters too would have a similar experience and, mind you, he did not take a complimentary service. He paid for the three haircuts.

This was a massive learning experience for all of us. I share this story with my team members on several occasions. It shows us how the underprivileged also aspires to connect with our brand and how by offering affordable services we can also service the marginalized sections of our society. It is important that we keep on doing the good work. Even if it is not promoted or marketed or advertised, potential customers notice it, and the efforts will be rewarded. The other significant aspect is how we reached out to a larger section of the masses, unknowingly. Even in JH HairXpreso we continued with the same price for a long time. It was only in 2016 that we increased the price from ₹99 to ₹149. However, for the kids, the price remained at ₹99 per haircut. Despite the rise in the price tag, we have still remained within the reach of that segment of the market for whom a haircut at Jawed Habib is something to boast of even if they can afford it only, probably, once a year.

JH HairXpreso is a game changer in the history of India's wellness sector. Across the country, it created a new segment with its fast, modern and contemporary dry haircuts at low prices. In other words, JH HairXpreso brought designer haircuts within the affordability of the common man. It also aimed at the Indian youth who will not mind paying ₹149 for a good haircut as it would not pinch his pocket much.

Marketing experts will prefer to call this strategy of mine as mass marketing. What is it? If I go by the conservative definition, mass marketing means a marketing strategy whereby a large section of the market is targeted without taking into consideration the normal demographic differences. The aim is to reach out to the largest number of audience and the business plan is to focus on high sales even at lower

First Floor, East Block, Amanora Tower Centre, Hadapsar, Pune

price points. This strategy is effective when someone is dealing with a product that is needed by different sections of society. It is precisely opposite to the niche marketing approach. There are certain distinct disadvantages to mass marketing and the most prominent among these is that with time the consumer interest in the product slowly ebbs out. They are tired of an all-inclusive approach that is generally associated with mass marketing.

For me, a haircut is a service that is taken by the masses, so I had to opt for a mass-marketing strategy. But I have never tried to fit everyone in one salon. I have consciously created different brands for different segments and different geographies of the market. My business module of franchising is also aimed at roping in as many partners possible. This helps me in reaching out to more people by dividing and sharing the ownership of the brand. I too have an all-inclusive approach but not one particular model that will suit all. This has helped me to negate the disadvantages of a mass module of business.

ANALYSING THE POTENTIAL FRANCHISEE

Even while selecting a franchisee, I do not only look at the financial stability of the partner like many firms are known to do. My advice to my team is to understand the passion of a potential franchisee, whether he or she thinks like us. If the thought process is the same, we can take the team to newer heights building upon each other's strengths. Inculcation of the Jawed Habib work culture among the team members is extremely important. And when I say team, it comprises head-office staff, master franchisees, franchisees, hairdressers, beauticians, shampoo boys and the support staff too.

Several of my existing franchisees are either working in my salons or had worked earlier with us. There are stories of young boys entering my salons as a shampoo boy, and then they undertook hairdressing courses and became hairdressers. Later, they have taken our franchisee too and have become a salon owner but remained with the brand. This too is an *aam aadmi* model of doing business. These young people are the true flag-bearers of the Jawed Habib brand. It also proves how our organization has changed the course of an individual's life from an unskilled labour to a successful entrepreneur. This has happened because I deliberately focused on the large section of the Indian middle class and not restricted my view only to the urban elite.

However, one distinct necessity for running a mass model of business is to remain connected with the masses. With success, if I had alienated myself from the common masses of this country, I would not have been able to build a network of 850 plus salons. Even today, when I wish to increase this number by many more times, I ensure that I am always in touch with them. For this, I do three things mentioned in the following sections.

MASS MARKETING VIA SOCIAL ROUTE

I am extremely active on social media. My YouTube channel has over 5 lakh subscribers. My Facebook page, Jawed Habib Hair Expert, is followed by over 6 lakh people and liked by another 4 lakh. So, are my Instagram and LinkedIn profiles. I constantly share my personal phone number with my students and clients so that I can solve their professional, educational and hair-related problems. Through WhatsApp also, I regularly keep in touch with the masses.

WORKSHOPS

I regularly attend workshops where I either aspire, hairdressers or professionals, who have already established themselves and who participate to learn from me new techniques and fashion trends. It is a knowledge-sharing session. I learn from the participants too. On average, I attend at least 50 such workshops in a year, roughly four a month. So, even by a conservative estimate, if say 150 hairdressers attend a workshop, I actually meet 600 new hairdressers ever month or 7,500 every year. I can easily relate myself with them because I am a hairdresser too. They can also understand what I am talking about. This connects two of us.

TRAVEL

This brings me to the third important aspect. It is my travelling. For seminars and workshops, I travel to every nook and corner of this country. I never ever hesitated about the location of a seminar or my remuneration. I am always ready to go. Out of the 30 days in a month, I travel at least 20 days. The mode of travel is not a barrier for me. I do not mind travelling in a normal economy class on a flight. I am ready to take any train if flight is not an option. If needed, I travel on road for hours and even in local cabs. I have my refreshments at any roadside dhaba. I love to mingle with people, be it at airports, railway stations or bus terminuses. In fact, I love to have people around me always. They inspire me. They help me to stay relevant. They help me stay connected. They are my energy boosters. Kids love me a lot too. Whenever I do not work, I feel low. If I do not travel for some days, I feel lethargic. To avoid such situations, I am always on the road, meeting people, sharing my knowledge, floating my business ideas and taking feedback.

This is the mantra behind the success of my business which focuses only on the masses. The common man of this country is exceptionally knowledgeable and exceedingly affectionate towards me. I have received their love and care. In an effort to reciprocate and give back the warmth that I have earned over the years, I wish to work in such a manner that citizens of India become fashionable and my fellow hairdressers are respected like any other professional in this society. It is not a business strategy. It is my emotion. This is my innermost desire—my dream. If business happens, so be it.But none can take my dream away from me. I will continue to do whatever it needs to fulfil my dream. It ticks inside me eternally like the hands of the clock. When anything goes wrong, I immediately erase the memories as we do for our hard disks on the computer. I am fresh again next day. It is always a new morning for me.

I am not a celebrity hairdresser either I am a hairdresser of celebrities. However, whenever anyone comes in contact with me or visits my salons, they are treated like celebrities because they deserve such treatment. No matter what price they pay, it is always a value for their money. This is my common-man model of doing business.

TAKING THE LEAP INTO FRANCHISING

CHAPTER SIX

ONLY THOSE WHO WILL RISK GOING TOO FAR CAN POSSIBLY FIND OUT HOW FAR ONE CAN GO.

T. S. ELIOT

From the middle of the 1990s till date, which is almost a quarter of a century's time, the Indian industry has witnessed tremendous changes in all aspects and so too in the salon sector. Earlier, we used to have two different entities: one for men and the other for women. The concept of unisex salons was hardly present. For men, it was a salon where one used to get a haircut, hair dye, shave, trimming and some rudimentary pedicure, manicure and facial services. Good salons used to be air-conditioned with uniformed well-dressed staff and floors free of hair and dirt.

For women, it used to be beauty parlours. Housed in a world closed from outside, inside it used to be an all-women's affair. Skincare used to be primary business, followed by haircare. Haircuts were, probably, the least of the revenue generators. There used to be a few unisex salons, but their numbers were so negligible that they hardly left any impact on the market. However, there was one thing in common. Most of these salons and parlours were headed by an individual, the lead barber or the main beautician, and he or she had a team providing the services. The salons and the parlours used to be named after them. Every locality in any Indian city had a handful of such salons and beauty parlours. These units had their own committed clientele and they used to swear by their service provider. The relationship was more than what it is between a technician and a client. Sometimes the relationship crossed generations too. Father and son or mother and daughter both visited the same salon year after year. It was also noticed that the same technician kept on working for years and then the knowledge was passed on to their sons and daughters. We have grown up seeing the industry in this format.

A Jawed Habib Hair & Beauty Salon at Lucknow

This was the primitive form of the Indian salon industry. It was highly unorganized or rather totally disorganized. Individual excellence was restricted to a single centre. Sharing of knowledge, skill and expertise were limited within families. Success stories were not replicated and failures kept on repeating. Modern practices were not adopted. Hygiene was hardly considered important. The primary and only recipe of success as an individual's brilliance.

However, economic liberalization ushered in the winds of change. Two things happened simultaneously. First, with the rise in income levels, mostly within the middle and upper-middle classes of the Indian society, the demand for salon services increased phenomenally. Second, economic liberalization brought

Jawed Habib Salon's Reception Counter at GIP Mall, Noida, Uttar Pradesh

the West, primarily Europe, closer to India. There too, the salon industry evolved from an individual-centric single unit to an institution-led format. The successful Indian technicians, when exposed to this world, realized their shortcomings. They understood that to survive they would have to grow and change. So, with their intelligence and entrepreneurial ability, they started bringing in changes which in reality became a paradigm shift for the entire Indian salon industry.

Openness in a salon's ambience, regular and coordinated exchange and sharing of knowledge and expertise, replication of successful models and building salon chains, hiring experts from other industries, accepting and implementing modern managerial practices and focusing on hygiene parameters, giving importance to customer feedback are just to name a few of the phenomenal changes that the industry has witnessed over the past few years. There are many more and there will be even more, but the fundamental transformation that has occurred is that the industry is now being led by institutions rather than by individuals.

THIS TRANSFORMATION IS BEST EXEMPLIFIED IF ONE FOLLOWS THE GROWTH OF INDUSTRY LEADERS OF THIS INDUSTRY. THEY ARE LEGENDS IN THEIR OWN RIGHT. THEY ARE SUCCESSFUL NOT JUST AS TECHNICIANS BUT AS ENTREPRENEURS.

They have created the Indian salon industry. Through their hard work, dedication, commitment and faith in their abilities, they first created their own niche areas, and then they did the most difficult task of changing themselves and their style of operation. As a result, their organizations grew from being driven by an individual to one driven by an institution.

All of them may not have a pan-India presence, but many are working in that direction. This change is not over because change does not end. It is a movement along a path which also witnessed the entrance of multinational companies (MNCs) into this market. These companies were primarily used to be product manufacturers. They wanted their own niche space or a salon where they could showcase their entire product range. So, these MNCs started selling beauty services to enhance the consumption of their existing and future products.

Along with them, another bunch of players entered the Indian market. They were primarily service sellers. Their expertise was in providing quality service irrespective of the products they used. These players are leaders in their respective geographies and are now eager to have a share of the fast-growing Indian market too. The presence of two such types of companies in the Indian salon industry has made the Indian market extremely competitive. These two players are Tony & Guy and Vidal Sassoon.

As a result of these developments, the Indian salon industry has become an interesting melting pot where local expertise is exposed to global competition, and the multinational players, despite their huge successes abroad, are finding the Indian market difficult as to where to leave their footprints. In the meantime, another interesting development has happened. The Indian salon sector is no longer individual driven. It is now witnessing a fight between several established corporate organizations. In fact, Indian industrial history has witnessed the same transformation too. From individuals such as Jamsetdji Tata or Ghanshyamji Birla or Dhirubhai Ambani we have now grown and created corporate bodies such as Reliance or Tata Sons or the several Birla and Goenka companies.

Desi wellness companies are no longer proprietorship or partnership firms. Equity investors play a significant role. Along with them, the venture capitalists are taking up strategic stakes in these leading Indian firms and more will be witnessed in future. This move will then culminate in public offering of equity shares of the Indian salon giants. Once that happens, institutions of the Indian salon industry will be owned not by the founder individuals but by the Indian masses, financial institutions and others. This is the way forward and we will witness it soon.

Who knows, in future, we may have an L&T in this industry too. L&T Ltd, the multi-billion-dollar engineering, construction and manufacturing company, was earlier known as Larsen & Toubro Ltd. In 1938,

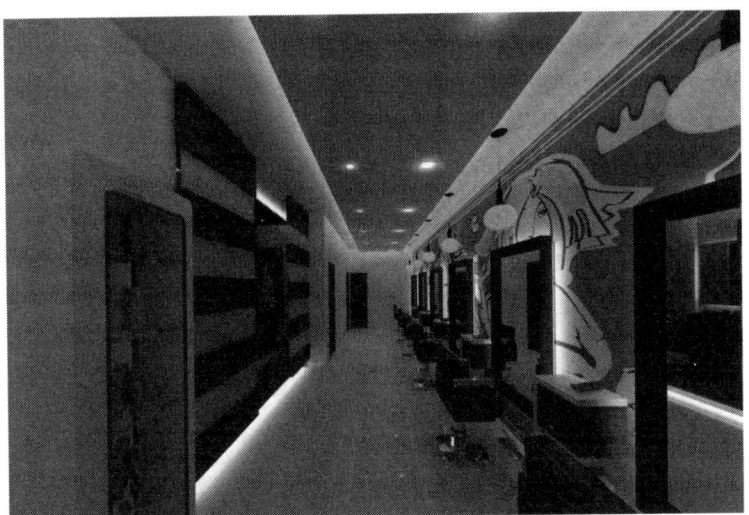

Swanky Interior of the Hair & Beauty Salon at Vishnupuri, Indore, Madhya Pradesh

two Danish engineers, Henning Holck-Larsen and Soren Kristian Toubro, started this firm in Mumbai. They are no more. Today, neither they nor any of their family members are in the management team. Even if they hold any stake, it is just like a common shareholder, but the company has grown to become a leader. This is the ultimate destination for any organization which moves from an individual entity to becoming an institution.

The growth of the Indian salon industry would not have been possible if the concept of franchising was not injected into it. It would not be wrong in any way if I say that I was the first to introduce it in this sector. I started off with the partnerships where we worked on different models of revenue sharing, but since 2009

Well Spaced Out JH Salon at Xion Square Mall, Hinjawadi, Pune

it has only been franchising. Ours is an organization which solely follows this path for expansion. Prior to 2009, we had extensively worked on the FOCO (franchisee-owned but company-operated) and COCO (company-owned and company-operated) models. We know the ins and outs of these models. After these experimentations, we finally settled down on the franchising model.

What is franchising? The management books describe it as a time-barred relationship between a master or a parent company, which is called the franchisor, and a follower company, the franchisee. Here the franchisor shares or provides a licensed privilege to the franchisee to conduct business and it also helps the franchisee through trainings, merchandising, marketing and promotion of the licensed product or service. Against this, the franchisor takes money within the ambit of certain terms and conditions. In other words, franchising is a form of business expansion where the owner (franchisor) of a product or service or a method or a concept gains new territories and markets through the affiliated dealers, the franchisees. Essentially, a franchisee pays an initial fee and then royalties to the franchisor during the franchising period for the ongoing support from the franchisor and for the right to use the franchisor's name, its way of doing business or for selling its products and services.

This is probably the crudest definition that can be given to this unique model of business as it misses out on the ethos and the spirit of this model. The relationship that is shared between the franchisor and the franchisee is not explained here. It does not begin with the payment of fees or extended with the monthly royalties. A successful relationship between a franchisor and a franchisee lies in the mutual bonding which is hard to describe in words.

Several books have been written on the concept of franchising, its successes and failures, its advantages and disadvantages. Like several other things, this model too has come from developed economies. I will not go into such details. Instead, I will share the experience of my journey through the world of franchising.

Just to put some facts straight. At present, when I am writing this book, by this I mean in June 2019, we have 864 salons spread over 121 cities in 24 Indian states. All these stores are franchises, barring one in New Delhi. I consider all these stores, mine. Any day I can work in any of these salons as a hairdresser.

> FOR ME, THERE IS NOTHING AS A FRANCHISEE STORE BECAUSE ALL THESE SALONS CARRY MY BRAND NAME JAWED HABIB. MY NAME IS THE BRAND.

SHIFTING FROM PARTNERSHIP TO FRANCHISEE

Now, why did I shift from the partnership mode of operations to the franchisee mode? I have often faced this question. The answer is simple. It was the issue of scalability. The partnership model was not scalable. It worked perfectly fine when we had around 50–60 salons. From there onwards as we kept on increasing the numbers of salons, managing the network from a central head office was becoming difficult. I realized that this model can sustain a maximum of around 100 salons and not beyond that. So, I had to shift from the partnership model to the franchisee mode of operations.

The year was 2009. I was operating with two brands, Jawed Habib Hair & Beauty salons and Jawed Habib Hair Academy. I decided to give master franchisee rights for these two brands for certain geographies.

For those who do not know what a master franchisee means, it is a franchising contract where the parent company or the master franchisor hands over the control of the franchising operations in a particular region or geography or a specific territory to a particular individual or an entity. This entity is called the master franchisee who controls the franchising operations of that particular region and becomes the representative of the master franchisor in that region. In other words, the master franchisee is supposed to be a mirror reflection of the master franchisor. He is supposed to play a pivotal role in the growth of the master franchisee in that territory. In short, the master franchisee is a mini master franchisor of that region. Within that territory, the master franchisee recruits, trains and provides ongoing support to each franchisee they sign.

Today, whatever it may appear or whatsoever is the perception of our franchisee operations, 10 years back it was not easy to sell the concept of master franchising. The existing partners were not too eager to become either a franchisee or a master franchisee for two reasons. One was obviously the comfort zone they were in. In the partnership model, the primary ownership remained with the parent company and all the employees were on the company's rolls. The partners were not eager to take up this responsibility. Moreover, even in the bad months when the bottom line of the salon or its profitability was hit, they were not affected because they had their share from the top line—the turnover. In short, they were insulated against the vagaries of business and that was their comfort zone. It was a safe investment for them without much involvement in daily operations. The second factor was the lack of knowledge of franchising. The partners thought that the company was alienating itself from the existing salons. They apprehended that they would be left to fend for themselves in difficult times. They hardly saw the opportunity that was ahead.

BOTTLENECKS ARE BLESSINGS IN DISGUISE

I distinctly remember offering master franchisee rights to those among the existing partners who I felt would be able to deliver and take the business to the next level. Among them, two turned it down. The price that I asked for was a throwaway one. Even then, they did not agree. Why I do not know. Maybe they thought that this model would not work. Or maybe they felt that there was not enough scope to grow the business. It was a boon in disguise. The new ones who came in gave the fillip that I was looking for. They understood what I wanted from them. They believed in my dream and worked hard in the expansion of our salon network.

There is a common tendency among many franchisees and master franchisees. Whenever I cited an example of success to them, they had this odd habit of saying that it was not possible in their region because it was not as developed as the one discussed. I agree that this country of ours is so big and diverse that the demographics changes every five kilometres. Manipur is different from Maharashtra, I know. I also agree that the market dynamics at Ambala in Punjab is different from Anantapur in Andhra Pradesh. Yes, the tastes and festivals of Kolkata are different from Kolhapur. Siliguri and Surat are two distinctly different cities. I am aware of all these. Even then I strongly believe that the basic tenor of all regions and cities and states are the same.

What is that? Indians know the value of money. They can differentiate a good service from a bad one. They feel the warmth of hospitality. They are more comfortable with the local players, and finally, the brand Jawed Habib is known across the country and what the brand offers or the value of the brand is also well known. This is the factor that unites all regions and cities of this country for the Jawed Habib salons. The moment a franchisee or a master franchisee realizes it, success opens its doors for them. For the past two and a half decades, I have worked really hard and travelled across the length and breadth of this country to build this brand value. All that I do each and every day is actually a work in that direction. Retain the value of the Jawed Habib brand and then enhance it further. I know what I have achieved and I have my eyes set on what I wish to achieve. My critics may defer with me, but even the severest of them cannot criticize me on the efforts that I have put in.

However, all my partners were not as disparaging as the others. Some of them believed in my dream. They trusted in what I shared with them. They also felt that there is a huge market that can be tapped for growth. They followed the path I showed them. They also worked equally hard like me to expand the network of salons.

TRUST MAKES THE WORLD GO ROUND

The most important thing that is required for a successful franchise operation is trust. Like all relationships, here too, faith and trust are the two most important needs. At present, I run a three-tier organization. On the top, there is the corporate office, below it is the master franchisees and then further down are the franchisees. There should be trust and transparency among all the three tiers. The head office, which I feel is the central nervous system, should understand the needs of all the franchisees. They should also feel their pains. So, whenever a policy is being framed or a new working structure is being prepared, they should keep in mind what would be its ramifications even at the lowest end of the strata, maybe for a salon located at Sidhi in Madhya Pradesh or Gaya in Bihar or Bahadurgarh in Haryana or Deoria in Uttar Pradesh or Kakinada in Andhra Pradesh or Vapi in Gujarat or Karad in Maharashtra to name a few. A decision taken at the head office affects the lives of 25 master franchisees, 800 franchisees and almost 10,000 technicians and non-technicians who are working in these salons. Therefore, every single decision is a tremendous responsibility on the team in Mumbai's corporate office. They are fully aware of it and are constantly in touch with me directly and also with the master franchisees and franchisees. The team feels the pulse of these entities and they make sure that they are never alienated. These 10,000 odd people are the roots of this massive banyan tree called Jawed Habib Hair & Beauty which is branching out to every *mohalla* (colony) of this country.

They earn the revenue like the roots which bring in the water and minerals from the soil for the tree. They keep the tree grounded against the wind and storm. My team members in all these unknown towns and cities too wither all the severities and give us the freedom to grow further.

In return, the franchisees must have faith and conviction in the plans and activities of the head office or the corporate headquarters. They should trust me. They should trust my decisions; believe that I will not do anything that will affect their interests. I will not take any step that will mar their future business prospects. Generally, it so happens that these technicians or the franchisees located at the small towns and cities or in some non-descript location view the business only from their perspective. Their vision is limited and restricted to that zone only. It is micro in nature. They are unable to look at the bigger picture; I do not blame them. Their business interests and exposure are limited. However, for me and the corporate office, it is a macro-view of the entire country and at times it goes beyond the boundaries of this nation. So, we have to take decisions which may not appear to be of any significance to them but, I know, that these will certainly help even the smallest player in the long run.

Let me give you an example. I regularly travel abroad for business expansion. We have salons in Bangladesh, Nepal and UAE. We will soon be opening salons in the UK, Kenya, Uganda and Tanzania. For a franchisee of Jawed Habib Hair & Beauty located at, say, Latur in Maharashtra or Shillong in Meghalaya, it may appear that it will not help them in any way. But they are wrong. Acceptability of brand increases with the rise in its presence in different markets. If I have a happy Kenyan customer of Jawed Habib Hair & Beauty and he/she is on a holiday in the hill town of Shillong and desperately wants a haircut, he/she will visit our salon because he/she knows us and knows the quality of our service. He/she will not prefer to try out anywhere else. This is a psychology of a customer and I am working on it. Mind you, this is also the reason behind the success of a KFC or a McDonald or a Pizza Hut all over the world. Their universal menu is a saviour for those travelling abroad but unable to adapt to the local cuisine. It means that customers connect with the brand. An affinity grows between the two. The comfort factor plays a crucial role. This helps a brand to grow.

I have cited just one example. There are many more. Like the Indian diaspora settled abroad or the Indian expatriates working in foreign countries. This is a huge population. An Indian brand which operates universally can touch the lives of this section of people quite easily. Recently, I travelled to Nairobi. Immediately after coming out of the Jomo Kenyatta International Airport, I looked for a local sim card for my cellphone.

There were several options, but the moment I saw Airtel, I opted for it because it is an Indian brand and I am aware of their services. So without giving it a second thought, I purchased their sim card and a user package. This is precisely what I am practising when it comes to our global presence. Gone are the days when Indians, both within the country and abroad, looked for international brands. Now they are happy to give their fellow citizens an opportunity because the Indian organizations are at par with the global standards, so are our Jawed Habib salons.

Going back to the trust factor between a franchisor and a franchisee I would like to add one more point. Both should understand that the ownership of the brand is now a shared entity.

> THE FRANCHISOR MAY HAVE CREATED THE BRAND BUT HE MUST REALIZE THAT SEVERAL INDIVIDUALS AND ENTITIES HAVE INVESTED MONEY, TIME AND ENERGY AS A FRANCHISEE TO MAKE IT GROW. LEGALLY, THE OWNERSHIP CAN ALWAYS BE RETAINED BY THE FRANCHISOR, BUT SPIRITUALLY IT IS OWNED BY THE FRANCHISEES TOO.

It is intangible and it cannot always be spelt out in a proper manner in a franchisee agreement. It is a fact. On the other hand, when a franchisee becomes a part of a big organization, he/she should realize that there are certain rules and regulations that he/she will have to adhere too. Just investing money does not give franchisees the freedom of doing whatever they wish to.

They can afford this luxury if they have started their own business with their own brand name. In a franchisee set-up, they should understand the rules of the game before getting onto the playing field.

FINANCIALS IN FRANCHISING

Coming to the aspect of an investment, I agree that the money that is being invested by the franchisees and the master franchisees help the company to grow. Even by a conservative estimate, the cost of setting up a salon today in India is around ₹25 lakhs, and if we are looking at 1,000 salons, the total investment will be around ₹250 crore to ₹300 crores. Add to it the total investment of the master franchisees in building the infrastructure for supporting the franchisees and the total investment will come to around ₹350 crores. This sum of money can be garnered from different sources. The avenues are known to all. A company can build its own chain of stores with these funds too. However, in this model, I will not have 700–800 bubbling entrepreneurs with me who are hardworking and equally passionate like me. They are hungry for success. They have a burning desire within them to prove that even with a small amount of money they can create their own enterprise. This is the biggest advantage of having a franchisee growth module against an organic plan of expansion.

On the other hand, for a franchisee with a minimum investment of ₹10–15 lakhs, they become a part of India's biggest wellness brand. They can afford to have a team of 50 professionals working in Mumbai for the betterment of their units. They can consider themselves to be a part of Jawed Habib Hair & Beauty Ltd. They can have Jawed Habib working in their salons too.

> THE GOOD PART ABOUT THE FRANCHISING MODEL OF OPERATIONS IS THAT BOTH THE PARTIES ARE WINNERS PROVIDED YOU HAVE THE RIGHT FRAME OF MIND AND A PROPER UNDERSTANDING OF THE MODEL. IT CAN WORK MIRACLES.

Today with great pride, I can say that I have franchisee partners who have worked with me in my salon as cleaning boys. Years back when they joined the salon, they neither had the money nor any expertise, but they had zeal. From cleaning the salons, they became shampoo boys. From there, they went to become either hairdressers or beauticians, and now they are my franchisee partners. Several of them own more than one franchisee. They are my brand ambassadors. They make me proud. Their success story is my success story. Their hard work and our business model have written several such success stories and I am sure more will be written in future. The franchise model is like sharing a helping hand, and once it is held firmly, no one fails, neither the one who is holding it out nor the one who is gripping it.

However, all is not hunky dory. There are several instances where we have failures. There are instances where the franchisee failed to look into the bigger aspects and remained confined to their self-interests only. Matters have gone to court too, but I think this is natural, and such instances are only an aberration. After all, only exceptions prove a rule.

On the whole, the franchising system has worked successfully for me and my organization. This is because I succeeded in selling a career and not a business proposition. Whosoever joins Jawed Habib Hair & Beauty, he or she has a dream of making it big in this world.

A shampoo boy graduates to become a hairdresser because he wants to be another Jawed Habib. In fact, most hairdressers in this country want to be a Jawed Habib. I firmly believe that they can be one if they join hands with me and follow me. They will have to listen to me and do what I am asking them to do. I have a success formula with me which I am ready to share with all the hairdressers of India. This country and this profession need more Jawed Habibs so that no one can even dare to look down upon us and say it is just a *nai ka kaam* (the job of a barber) in a derogatory manner. Franchising helps me achieve it.

SHARED OWNERSHIP

I do not know what a commune looks like or how it operates in an ideal situation. I am also not fully aware of a socialist dream of their society, but I strongly believe franchising, though an outright capitalist model of business operations, has a streak of socialism in it. The idea of shared ownership or the concept of involving all in the growth or the core policy of distributing expertise among those who cannot afford are the basic tenets of socialism, and all these are present in franchising. The model helps the franchisor to touch the geographies beyond the territories it can reach on its own and also helps the franchisee to summit the peaks of success as a mountain of resources are always at his or her disposal. This aspect of franchising has a sense of socialism in it because both the franchisor and the franchisee belong to the same working class.

In a country like India, franchising is the perfect model because it is inclusive in nature, so is my company Jawed Habib Hair & Beauty Ltd. Anyone, the skilled or the unskilled, an expert or a non-expert, a man or a woman, a trained hairdresser in a metro or an uneducated barber of a village, can be a part of my organization. Their gains will not just be theirs only or of my organization. Their achievements will be that of their society and the nation at large. Despite sounding repetitive, I must add that I strongly believe that the model of franchising will make India economically stronger.

MY INDIAN WAY OF MARKETING

CHAPTER SEVEN

A BRAND IS NO LONGER WHAT WE TELL THE CONSUMER IT IS—IT IS WHAT CONSUMERS TELL EACH OTHER IT IS.

SCOTT COOK

Have you ever done a google on salon marketing? You will find numerous websites giving you all sorts of ideas on the very first page. One link says, '31 Innovative Salon Marketing Ideas to Build your Clientele'. Another shouts, '65 Salon Marketing Ideas'. A third claims that it has '17 Hair-Raising Salon Marketing Ideas'. One other notes that it has '15 Salon Marketing Ideas' to get more customers.

There would be at least 100 such websites giving at least 20 ideas each. Think of the number of ideas that are available online with just a few clicks! I tried to read some of them just for the sake of reading, and after a point of time, I was totally confused despite the fact that most of the websites talk about the same points over and over again. After an hour or two of reading, I felt that I do not know anything on the subject of 'marketing of salon' even after building a network of around 900 salons.

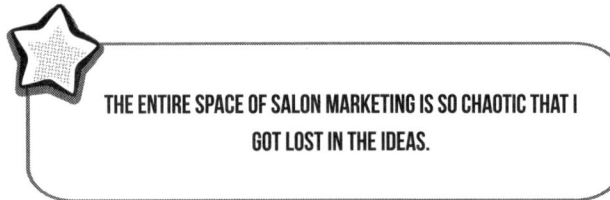

THE ENTIRE SPACE OF SALON MARKETING IS SO CHAOTIC THAT I GOT LOST IN THE IDEAS.

The famous words of Philip Kotler, who is considered the Father of Modern Marketing, came to my mind, 'Marketing takes a day to learn. Unfortunately, it takes a lifetime to master.' Nothing can be truer than this. This gentleman, who has been the International Marketing Chair Holder at Northwestern University for over three decades now, rightfully said that nowadays 'everybody markets something' but 'knowing how to market' is the challenge. In his autobiography *My Adventures in Marketing*, he writes,

> A marketer is someone who seeks a response—attention, a purchase, a vote, a donation—from another party, called the prospect. There are many things that can be marketed. They include not only *goods and services,* but also *events, experiences, persons, places, properties, organizations, information, ideas* and *causes.*

He gave the briefest and the most relevant definition of marketing, 'Marketing is about identifying and meeting human and social needs.' One of the shortest definitions of marketing is 'meeting needs profitably'.

MARKETING THE JH BRAND

There are several opinions and definitions available on marketing, its needs and significance in today's world of business by some of the global experts in this field. I have selected a few to elaborate further so that I can establish the way I have gone ahead with the activity of marketing my brand in the Indian market.

Julie Barile, who is considered an expert in e-commerce and digital marketing both for mass and luxury products and was associated with brands such as Avon and Club Monaco (owned by Ralph Lauren), has an interesting view on this matter. She feels that marketing is primarily a way by which a company communicates, connects and engages its target group to inform or convey the value of its product or service with the ultimate aim of selling it. She wrote:

> However, since the emergence of digital media, in particular social media and technology innovations, it has increasingly become more about companies building deeper, more meaningful and lasting relationships with the people that they want to buy their products and services. The ever-increasingly fragmented world of media complicates marketers' ability to connect and, at the same time, presents incredible opportunity to forge new territory.

I feel that marketing is a way by which we connect with products and services that we have to offer to the potential customers who need those products. This mode of communication is multi-dimensional. It starts with an understanding of the market and its needs. This understanding can come through research or with the company's connection with the market. The communication has to be created to inform the customers about the offering. It is a constantly evolving process. There is no fixed formula. The only formula is to stay connected with the market and with the target audience in that market.

It is through marketing by which an organization creates enterprise value where the brand name is the face and behind it lies business strategy and planning. To do that, an organization will have to be extremely specific about the sector of the market it is targeting.

Jawed Habib at the Headquarters of His Holiness the Dalai Lama at McLeodganj, Himachal Pradesh

Through marketing, the organization informs its target audience what it wishes to deliver and exactly how important it is for them. Marketing is the way one shares his story.

Marketing is also a way to educate the target audience. Mind you, educating a target audience is extremely important while introducing a new product or service. An uneducated audience will not appreciate the value of the product or the service. Effective education will create the need for a new product by igniting the desire for that product in the customers' mind. It is this education which has a far-fledged reach, so much so that it even made me meet personalities like Dalai Lama. This wouldn't have been possible without this marketing approach which made me a known face in every part of the country.

And to do that successfully, the enterprise will have to know its target audience extremely well. As I said, establishing a connection is essential. Once a relationship is established, the customer will start promoting your organization and product or service voluntarily. They will take pride in sharing your posts on social media or your newsletter among friends and family members.

Marketing is an umbrella term which covers research, branding, public relations activities, promotions, loyalty programmes, collection of direct response and staying connected with the audience. In fact, it is the art of creating, delighting and keeping your customers happy for a long span of time without hampering the profitability of the company. This, in short, is the creation of enterprise value.

UNRAVELLING THIS MARKETER'S JOURNEY

My journey of the last 25 years is actually a journey of a marketer. All that I have done in these years was aimed at creating a brand of mine and then marketing it within the masses. It was always clear in my mind that my target audience was the entire population of this country, and so I have been saying that I want to give a haircut to every one of them. Apart from this, I wanted to establish hairdressing as a respectable profession. Unfortunately, there was, and to some extent even today there is, a negative aspect of this work. I wanted to get rid of it. I knew that it could happen only when we had educated hairdressers and not just skilled barbers.

That was probably the reason why I had created the world record for the most number of haircuts. In 1997, I did 410 non-stop free haircuts in 27 hours and 18 minutes. My initial target was 24 hours, but I could not finish it within that time. I took a break of only one and a half hours. I was only 34 years of age at that time. It entered into the *Limca Book of Records*. This helped me to introduce hairdressing as a profession in that book. It created a furore in the market. All of a sudden people started taking note of the work done by hairdressers. Many saw it as a gimmick. A few days after that event, I remember, a journalist asked me whether

Jawed Habib with UP's Former Chief Minister Akhilesh Yadav for a Project on Skill Development

it was a publicity stunt. I only told her, 'It means a lot of hard work.' She agreed, and not only she but others too started realizing that hairdressing like any other profession required dedication, knowledge and hard work. Although unconsciously, still, I believe that this is the first step that I took in my marketing journey. Later on, this record might have been broken by others and new numbers would have been achieved. However, for me, the significance was not the number of haircuts I did but the buzz that I had successfully created. Even today, many people while introducing me, talk of that small achievement of mine. Hence, that 22-year-old act of mine is still making marketing wonders for me.

Apart from haircuts, spreading hair education is another thing that I have always loved to do. In fact, I am not too sure what I love doing most, working on clients or addressing students in a seminar or workshop. However, it is true that I never hesitated or ever felt tired of doing any of these works. Through these two activities, I did all my promotions, public relations activity and client base building. In short, it is marketing that I have done.

I have been conducting seminars, as I have said, for many years now. I started it probably in 1996 or 1997. Initially, it used to be week-long workshops where I used to give hands-on training to the participants. It started with 'how to hold a pair of scissors' and ended with chemical work. Initially, there used to be 10–15 students. Over the years, the number of students increased and at the same time, I got engaged with many other things too. So, I reduced the seminar time from seven to five and then to three days. At present, I only conduct one-day seminars. This is more of a see-and-learn activity. This sort of a seminar caters mostly for those who are in the industry for years but just needs a brushing up. Then I do the masterclasses where I personally give hands-on training to students who are learning the art of hairdressing. In all these classes, I have never promoted any product. I only tried to teach the students the science behind haircuts and hairdressing. I feel that if they can learn the basics of hairdressing properly, then they can work in any part of the world and with any product. Unfortunately, the multinational product manufacturers teach the students how to use their products and not the logic and science behind it.

The general practice in my seminars and workshops is that a student gets a participation certificate from the Jawed Habib Hair Academy and also gets an opportunity to take a photograph with me. Earlier, it used to be the analogue cameras. Nowadays everyone come with their smartphones. So, clicking a photograph has become easy. Today, a selfie is a must with a student. These photographs and certificates are of great value to these students. They treasure it. Mostly, they frame the pictures and the certificates and put it up in their salons.

MARKETING THROUGH CERTIFICATES OF PARTICIPATION

Several people have asked me why I am so generous in awarding the certificates from the Jawed Habib Hair

Academy. They felt that I am devaluing my institute and the certificate it issues. As a clarification, let me say that the certificates these students get are only a 'Certification of Participation' and nothing more. Second, when these certificates are framed and put up in local salons, the salons gain value. For those who enrol in our academies and successfully complete the courses get a different set of certificates. Hence, there is no confusion in that respect.

However, what many people do not see is the marketing that I do through these seminars. With the certificates and my framed photograph used in the local salons, the receivers of the certificates do not use my brand name, but they rather promote my brand. Whoever visits these salons will come to know of my brand name. Just imagine the number of people with whom I have connected just through this activity of mine. Let me give you an estimate. I generally do 50 seminars in a year and on average there are 100–150 students in a seminar. I have been conducting seminars for over the past 25 years. So, even if I consider that out of 150 students, only 100 have their own salons, then there are around 1,25,000 such certificates and photographs of mine in salons which I neither own and nor do they have my brand name, yet my brand is being promoted. Now if these salons have at least 100 footfall a month, which is only three per day, then around 1.25 crore people, which is just one per cent of the Indian population, have either seen my picture or the certificate issued by my academy. I hope now one can understand the enormity of the marketing work that I have done over these years.

Coming back to these salons where I have only picture and certificates, think of the situation from the customers' perspective. The clients in these salons, who I am sure are happy with the service they have received there, will take note that the person who has given the service has actually being trained by Jawed Habib. So, did I not get a higher and double appreciation? First, on the quality of the service he or she received and for training those able pair of hands. Second, the value of Jawed Habib gets further enhanced when a customer realizes that I have allowed my name to be used by the local hairdresser to get more clients, even though we are apparently competitors. This is a subtle way of marketing oneself and I have successfully done it.

Through the seminars, I have promoted my academies too. At present, there are 65 such academies in India. We garner students for these academies through these seminars. The attendees get a first-hand idea of how we go about training our students. It helps them to make a decision if they are doubtful of joining the Jawed Habib Hair Academy.

You will be surprised to know the places where I have conducted seminars. Itanagar in Arunachal Pradesh, Silchar in Assam, Midnapore in West Bengal, Port Blair in Andaman and Nicobar Islands and Jamshedpur in Jharkhand to name a few in the east. I think I have done similar seminars in all the cities of Punjab, Rajasthan, Haryana, Uttar Pradesh, Gujarat and Maharashtra. I have conducted seminars in Chennai too along with the cities of Kerala, such as Kochi and Thiruvananthapuram.

I have never seen whether I have a salon in that city or not. I am self-sufficient in these seminars. I just go there and address my fellow hairdressers. People generally say that language can be a barrier in India. I have never faced any such problem because I speak the language of hair with my fellow colleagues who are also hairdressers. They understand my language and I understand theirs.The process of imparting education or the act of exchanging knowledge, if done genuinely, is a great leveller. It brings both the giver and the receiver on the same podium where there are no differences of languages, class or status. That is why teaching is a noble profession and it will remain so.

BECOMING THE SCISSOR MAN OF INDIA

Like my seminars, I also did not hesitate to work in others' salons. I was never choosy. Years ago, it used to be a common practice of mine to work with clients wherever I visited. I never checked whether the salon had the right ambience or the perfect equipment because I just needed a pair of scissors to do a haircut. That's why I am called the Scissor Man of India. I am never finicky about such material things. I believe that to connect with a client as a hairdresser, I am always ready. Several hairdressers say that they do not work on other's clients or they work only in their salons. I do not have any such hassle. I feel these are idiosyncrasies of a hairdresser. As a doctor is always ready to attend a patient, so am I, always ready to attend to a client. 'Be open and be ready' is the motto of my life.

In fact, whenever I have travelled to a new city, where I do not have a Jawed Habib salon, to do a seminar, I have generally followed it up with haircuts in others' salons. I also make it a point to interact with as many people as possible, be it on the roads or markets or stations or airports. All these have helped me in promoting myself and my brand. In fact, over the years what we have noticed is that immediately after such a visit, we get franchisee enquiry calls from that city. So, these seminars, workshops and my working in others' salons have actually worked as roadshows for the promotion of my brand. Generally, corporate houses and other enterprises first create the infrastructure and then they go about doing the roadshows and promotions. Instead, I have done it the other way round. I have put the cart before the horse and it worked wonders. As a result, when we actually open a salon or introduce the academy, the market is ready. Customers and students are already educated about our services. They just walk in for a service or enrol for a course. This is an innovative marketing strategy of mine. No hairdresser would have ever thought of marketing himself/herself or his/her brand in this manner.

MARKETING THROUGH ASSOCIATE BODIES

It is not always easy to work in unknown territory. In several cities, there used to be associations of hairdressers and beauticians. Even today, there are many such local bodies. Although some of these associations have openly embraced me, there are several who have opposed my seminars and workshops. They tried to create obstacles. Some even went on to the extent of maligning me. They wanted their markets to remain insulated from me. They do such horrible things because they are insecure. They do not have confidence in their work. However, despite their best efforts, they could not stop me because wherever I went, I made more friends than enemies, and those friends have supported me all throughout.

Of late, another development is being noticed. Several salons are coming up with the tagline 'Trained by Jawed Habib'. Mostly these salons do not have a name. Even the words 'Trained by Jawed Habib' is displayed in such a manner that the words 'trained by' are hardly noticeable and the words 'Jawed Habib' are prominently showcased in higher and brighter fonts. It is a case of misusing my brand name. Training in any of my academies does not give anyone the right to use my brand name on their individual salon. Second, I think my education is sufficient and it empowers the technicians to such an extent that they can get clients on their own. There is no need to use my brand name as a parasite. Third, just by using my name, these unfortunate fellows are actually promoting my name. Instead, they should have tried to do it on their own. As we all know, there is no shortcut to success.

There are several fake salons too that use my brand name. One such salon has changed my name from JAWED to DAWEJ. I just fail to read the minds of people who are doing all this. Do they not realize that all this will not help them in the long run? Do they not understand that Indian customers know the difference? Why do they underestimate the knowledge of the Indian population? Indian customers are not fools. They are smart enough to identify the fake among the reals. I strongly feel that my community of hairdressers or the owners of such salons should stop doing it. They should be proud of their work and their brand name and put in all efforts to succeed. My legal team is always active in taking action against such offenders, but I think this should not have happened at all. This hurts me more as a hairdresser than as the owner of the Jawed Habib brand name, as I am a representative of this industry too. I have a simple message to all such hairdressers and salon owners. The Indian market is huge. There is much scope for growth for everyone. Give your best effort and you will be rewarded. If I can do it through hard work and dedication, you can do it too.

I may sound like sermonizing, but believe me, I am not doing so. I am just sharing my feelings. If it may sound so, I am helpless. The first and foremost agenda in my life is to raise the dignity of this profession. I believe that if Indian scientists, doctors, technocrats and IT professionals can create their niche in markets all over the world, so can our Indian hairdressers. Their calibre and ability are at par with the global leaders. They just need to shed such negative mindsets to progress further in their work.

Someone had told me that this is a marketing strategy of mine. I say these things to promote myself. I neither agree nor disagree with this thought because whenever I say such things, I say it from the core of my heart. I am 100 per cent honest about it. If people think differently, I cannot help it. But at the same time, many have read my honesty and have believed in me. My fellow hairdressers and salon owners, both technical and non-technical, know that Jawed Habib is actually promoting the industry and not himself.

I wish to touch upon another aspect of marketing, which is especially discussed in the context of India. This is called rural marketing. All big MNCs and even the Indian conglomerates look for ways to reach rural India. Reams and reams of study materials have been published on rural marketing. Some think of it as a huge challenge. For them, it is a big task to connect with the rural masses.

I do not think so. First, rural or urban, village or city, town or metro, whatever you call, it is India. No matter how diverse our nation is, there are certain things that are common all over. When our cricket team wins, all of us celebrate together. Whenever a heinous crime is committed, we protest together. In the case of a natural calamity, all Indians go out of their way to help the affected. Recently, the entire nation had cast their votes and exercised their franchisee for the new government. If such is the way of the life of our nation, why do we divide our marketing strategies?

BUILD ENGAGEMENT VIA SOCIAL MEDIA

Smartphones and technology have further united the country. I am an extensive user of this medium. Social media is a unifying factor, and over the past few years, I have used it extensively to market myself and my brand name.

I have seen the length and breadth of this country. Through my seminars and workshops, I have succeeded in meeting people from all sections of society. Some basic feelings and realizations are common everywhere. Languages, cultures and festivals may be different, but the entity is one. Durga Puja will remain the biggest festival in the East. Diwali will be for the North. Ganesh Chaturthi will remain the biggest crowd-puller of the West and Pongal for the South. It, however, does not mean that a Bengali will not burn crackers in Diwali. Pongal in Tamil Nadu means Nabanna in West Bengal. Vaisakhi in Punjab is celebrated around the Bengali New Year. Holi is celebrated with equal fervour all over the country. When it is Ramzaan, haleem is the most sought after dish of this nation, just like a plum cake is during Christmas.

As the head of Jawed Habib Hair & Beauty Ltd, I tell my team to understand the Indianness of this population which may have different hues, but in its core, it is the same. I would say one will have to feel it. Once it is felt, then creating a connection via social media platforms such as Facebook, Instagram and WhatsApp with the target audience is extremely easy. This is marketing for me—free of jargons, free of terminologies, free of concepts and free of strategies. Build an honest relationship and it will stay forever. Marketing becomes an easy activity once you understand what your customer wants and when you honestly try and deliver it. For me, marketing is all about honesty and hard work, and Indians respect it. Once you achieve it, your failures would be understood and not blatantly criticized.

To conclude, I will say, for me, marketing is building a relationship through different media with utmost sincerity and transparency.

GOING GLOBAL

CHAPTER EIGHT

THE EARTH IS A FINE PLACE AND WORTH FIGHTING FOR.

ERNST HEMINGWAY

Sometime back, Kofi Annan, the diplomat from Ghana, who was the seventh Secretary-General of the United Nations and also the Nobel Peace Prize winner of 2001, made an observation, 'It is being said that arguing against globalization is like arguing against the laws of gravity.' He further added that globalization is an 'irreversible process, not an option'.

In today's global economy, markets are no longer insulated with tariff or non-tariff barriers. Everyone is free to start operations in any geography. While leading multinational national companies (MNCs) have started operations in India, our domestic leaders are also foraying into global markets. It is happening in all the sectors.

JAWED HAS SET UP NUMEROUS SALONS AND ACADEMIES ACROSS INDIA AND THE GLOBE.

There are several success stories on either side. According to a survey, the leading MNCs who have huge operations in India are Microsoft, IBM, Nestle, Procter & Gamble (P&G), Coke, PepsiCo, Citi Group, Sony Corporation, HP and Apple. All these companies have not only created huge employments but have also succeeded in creating an enterprise value in India. On the other hand, Indian companies such as the Tata Group, the Aditya Birla Group, Bharti Airtel, HCL Technologies, Wipro, Infosys Technologies and ONGC, a public sector company, are doing extremely well abroad.

In his report to the General Assembly held in Paris on 1 October 1999, Mr Kofi Annan noted:

> In a globally integrated marketplace, both developing and developed countries need to accept greater responsibility, transparency and accountability in

policy-making. Globalization of the economy implies globalization of responsibility and response capacity. But governments alone or even together cannot deliver without the cooperation of such key actors in the global economy as the private sector and the civil society.

Mr Kofi Annan's views on the subject of globalization are extremely significant. As someone coming from a developing country, he was aware of the insecurities of these nations and, as the head of the United Nations, he played a crucial role to see that globalization became an inclusive phenomenon. Otherwise, the acceptability

Jawed Habib's Tie-up with International Brand Wella at P&G Office, London (Wella Was Owned by P&G from 2003 and Was Later Sold to Coty, Inc. in 2015)

of the transnational corporations would not have been easy. The view of leading economists and management gurus was focused on the corporations' gains and challenges, but he pointed out the human aspect of this global phenomenon.

STRATEGY FOR INTERNATIONAL MARKETS

Understanding the main difference between Indian and international markets is important. The Indian market is segregated by states, but foreign markets are segregated by countries. The first step here is to identify a country's master franchisee to take the brand to the local levels.

In India, although there is a growing awareness of the clinical and scientific approach, still it is in its nascent stage; this is more so in Western countries. So, these markets cannot be just driven by beauty and hair services. There was a need for holistic grooming involving clinical methods. Europe and the United States have more organized players as they are already established markets.

CUSTOMIZING AS PER THE INTERNATIONAL MARKETS

We combined our knowledge with the local market conditions and filled in the requisite gaps through our products and services.

We realized that we could penetrate these markets on the basis of some alternative therapies for rejuvenation which have eventually turned out to be an important revenue generator.

For me, personally, this was very important. As the head of Jawed Habib Hair & Beauty Ltd, I am always looking to expanding my network and building my business. Overseas markets are always a lucrative opportunity. However, how and where to go are significant factors. Presently, I have two salons in Bangladesh (one in Dhaka and the other in Chittagong) and one each at Kathmandu in Nepal and at Dubai in United Arab Emirates. As this book is being written, I have already finalized my plans for starting operations in Nairobi in Kenya. We are planning to open a Jawed Habib & Beauty salon and a Jawed Habib Hair Academy shortly. Work on this project has started. While this plan has already been

Going Global

firmed up, we are also looking at markets like Uganda in Africa and the United Kingdom.

EVALUATION STRATEGY

A company needs to evaluate whether or not expansion is indeed beneficial, and if it is beneficial, then how one should go about it and which countries should be targeted first.

EXPLORING OPPORTUNITIES IN NEIGHBOURING COUNTRIES

The strategy is simple. First, we explore the opportunities in our neighbouring countries. We are already there in Nepal and Bangladesh. We are scouting for partners in Sri Lanka, Bhutan and Myanmar, primarily the South Asian Association for Regional Cooperation (SAARC) countries. These markets, I feel, are the low-hanging fruits. Because of our similarities, I am confident that we will succeed soon.

> AS A PART OF YOUR STRATEGY, YOU SHOULD FIRST FOCUS ON THE LOW-HANGING FRUITS, SOMETHING THAT IS MORE ACCESSIBLE AND THEN GROW YOUR PRESENCE AND DIVERSIFY FURTHER.

TARGETING COUNTRIES WITH 'THE COMMON FACTOR'

After striking a chord with the neighbouring countries, our next focus area will be Europe. By Europe, I mean the United Kingdom and by the United Kingdom, I mean London. That is the market to be in. Being a former colony of the British, we still have several commonalities. For an Asian organization and brand name like mine, success in this market is the key. Once we succeed in London, I think the way forward will be the other European countries. I know the journey is not easy, but I am sure that it will start in London, and then it will move forward. I have already prepared an extensive plan for Europe.

TARGETING MARKETS WITH LESSER COMPETITION

Africa is a surprise beginning for me. My partner working in Kenya got in touch with me through Facebook. Thereafter things are moving smoothly. I have already conducted a workshop for the hairdressers of Kenya. I have also worked in some of the salons in Nairobi. This partner of mine is so confident that he wishes to spread the network all over East Africa and the other East African nations such as Uganda, Tanzania, Rwanda, Burundi and South Sudan.

Over the years, along with my expansion activities in India, my team and I also concentrated on the overseas market. I tried everything, from organic growth to franchisee operations. Not many people know, but I had acquired a salon-cum-training centre brand in Malaysia. The brand operated primarily in Kuala Lumpur. It did not work. I will not call it a failure because I learnt many a lesson ongoing global from this experience.

NEVER TRY TO COPY AN INDIAN COMPETITOR'S BUSINESS MODEL IN A FOREIGN COUNTRY.

I took my Indian technicians to these markets and wished that they settled there. However, it did not work in the manner I expected. Every nation has its own practices and cultures. To succeed in that market, one will have to market ourselves as a part of them. In Hindi, there is a popular saying, *'jaisa desh, waisa bhesh'*. It is the same like 'when you are in Rome, do as the Romans do'. It is important. If not followed, success will elude you.

Second, I wish to expand myself not as a company offering salon services. It is not a sustainable approach. This approach has not worked in the past and it will also not work in the future. Instead, I wanted to establish Jawed Habib Hair & Beauty as an Indian academy that imparts skills for this industry. This is my roadmap for the overseas market.

Why? First and foremost, any salon in this world can function smoothly if it has trained manpower. In India too, we may have around 900 salons, but the engines that run these salons are my 64 Jawed Habib Hair Academies. So, when I am venturing into a new market, I will have to ensure that I have the necessary manpower to run the salons, and for that, I need to get the locals get trained. I have already done it successfully in India. Even when we were starting our expansion in our own market, we tried to send hairdressers from Delhi to other parts of the country. They were reluctant. Some could not say no to me and moved, but I sensed that they were not comfortable. I knew to succeed, I would have to open training academies in every region of India with local talent. We did precisely that, and today all our salons have local hairdressers but trained at the Jawed Habib Hair Academy.

I feel that this strategy works for overseas markets. I plan to introduce my organization as a hair and beauty training academy and not as a salon service provider. The training schools will be the foundation of my business. To have a strong business mechanism, I will have to build a strong foundation. To have a fully blooming garden or an orchard full of fruits, one must have a nursery that nurtures the saplings and helps them grow into robust plants and trees.

The strategy is also to grow through acquisitions. I am always on the lookout for an acquisition of a chain of salons that can be moulded into our vision. It can be 10, 20, 30 or 40 salons. There are some plain and simple advantages of an overseas acquisition. Starting a business is easy; however, growing it usually becomes harder once a company has reached a certain point. One of the best ways of growing an existing company is through mergers and acquisitions. However, it is also worth noting that mergers and acquisitions are regulated in countries all over the globe, and they come with many advantages. Tax implication is an important factor. In some countries, an acquirer, if it is a foreign body, gets some tax advantages. An acquisition helps a company in getting a market share in a foreign country easily and instantly which is difficult if the company is following the organic growth path. For companies in our sector, these are the two most prominent advantages.

The merger of cultures, however, is a different and difficult ball game. Any organization, no matter where it operates, has its own set of practices and systems. It tends to continue with it and tries to introduce it in the newly acquired organization. Leaders of the acquiring companies think that they have the best practices available to them, and they tend to ignore and overlook the ones being followed by the acquired organization. This is not the right thing to do. An acquirer should have an open and balanced view of both the practices. They should also keep in mind the rationale behind the practices followed in the acquired company. Then using the best possible judgement, the acquiring company should bring the changes if at all it is necessary. There are several stories of acquisitions failing because cultures and practices of the two merging organizations are not compatible. Hence, while considering an acquisition along with business strategy and finances, the cultural aspect must be studied seriously too.

There is an Indian conglomerate with interests in varying industries such as cement, textiles, cellular services, mining and retailing. It is present in over 35 countries. The organization is extremely employee-friendly too. It has staff canteens in all its establishments where vegetarian food is served to employees at a cheap rate. In their initial years of expansion, they started the same practice in the companies they acquired. It included foreign acquisitions too. However, they noticed that the canteen or the food served there was not happily accepted by a large section of the employees in these foreign countries. On investigation, it was found that vegetarian food was not liked by them. In fact, the disgruntlement reached such a level that they had to allow non-vegetarian food in the office canteens. Organizations do face such insignificant but crucial issues post a merger or acquisition. Being aware of these factors and thinking through such issues are crucial for a successful merger or acquisition.

Most Indian salons venturing out into overseas markets have a common tendency. The companies mostly target the Indian expatriates or the Indian diaspora. According to the UN World Migration Report of 2018, the Indian diaspora is the world's largest, with slightly more than 15.6 million people from India living overseas. The report was released by the International Organization for Migration. The Indian diaspora constitutes 6 per cent of the total number of international migrants (people living outside the country of their birth), which was estimated at 243 million in 2015. The same report stated that Mexico has the second-largest diaspora after India. Russia and China are in the third and fourth positions, respectively. Our neighbours Bangladesh and Pakistan are in the fifth and sixth positions, respectively.

According to a report prepared by our team during our market research, it was found that in Nepal itself there are 4 million Indians, which is approximately 13–14 per cent of its population. Similarly, in Saudi Arabia, this size is 3 million, which is around 10 per cent of that nation's population. Even if we look at Malaysia, there are 2.4 million Indians. Now, let us look at Europe. In the United Kingdom itself, the number of Indians are over 14.5 lakhs and around 1.5 lakhs stay in Italy and the Netherlands. The United States of America, probably, has the highest number of Indians. There, the size of the Indian population is approximately 31–32 lakhs. In Canada, there are 12 lakh Indians. Even in Trinidad and Tobago, the Indian population is over 5 lakhs. Africa and South America are no exceptions. In South Africa, there are 1.3 million Indians which is approximately 2.7 per cent of its population. Mauritius has around 9 lakhs. It is hard to believe that in Guyana there are over 3 lakh Indians which is over 40 per cent of their population. In Australia, this number is around 4 lakhs and around a lakh in New Zealand.

Hence, it is all but natural for Indian companies to target this community. In most cases, this section of the population is aware of the Indian brands, and it is expected that there will be a natural affinity to the Indian players. I feel that these are the low hanging fruits for the Indian corporations overseas. However, if the companies only focus on this section, then I feel that it will not be the right approach.

I firmly believe that targeting the Indian diaspora in an overseas operation should only be a short-term measure, as over a long period of time it will not be a sustainable model. Ultimately, the Indian companies will have to create a connection with the local citizens of that country. The company will have to be a part of a nation's overall structure to succeed within its boundaries. They will have to win the hearts of everyone.

Have we ever thought of Philips being a Dutch company while buying its products? When we were young and our parents took us to a Bata store to buy a pair of shoes, we never knew that Bata is a Canadian company and that it started off as T&A Bata Shoe Company way back in 1894 at the Moravian town of Zlin (now in Czech Republic) by Thomas Bata. It did not happen because these companies and their products became part of Indian life. Indians valued their products. They trusted it more than many of its Indian competitors. There lies the success of an overseas venture. The consumer of a product or a service looks for the value of his or her money and when a corporation succeeds in delivering it repeatedly, over and over again, then it wins the heart of the consumer. Once it is done, success is bound to knock at its door.

So, from the perspective of Jawed Habib Hair & Beauty, my approach to going global is to establish my organization as a knowledge-based institution that imparts skills and knowledge of certain systems and processes to deliver proper quality salon services. When you have such a goal in mind, the target audience and geographies become immaterial. I will approach the overseas as I have done in the national market.

The success from the Bangladesh, Nepal, United Arab Emirates and Kenya markets make me confident in venturing into the other unexplored markets and as they say 'The Sky is the Limit'. I have a blue ocean in front of me. My vision is to make Jawed Habib Hair & Beauty a true Indian transnational wellness company.

GIVING BACK TO THE SOCIETY

CHAPTER NINE

LET US NOT SEEK THE REPUBLICAN ANSWER OR THE DEMOCRATIC ANSWER, BUT THE RIGHT ANSWER. LET US NOT SEEK TO FIX THE BLAME FOR THE PAST. LET US ACCEPT OUR RESPONSIBILITY FOR THE FUTURE.

JOHN F. KENNEDY

> AFTER SPENDING OVER 25 YEARS OF MY LIFE IN PUBLIC AND WORKING CLOSELY WITH SEVERAL GOVERNMENTS BOTH AT THE CENTRE AND IN THE STATES AND PERSONALLY KNOWING MANY POLITICAL LEADERS, OF WHICH QUITE A FEW ARE MY CLIENTS TOO, I HAVE RECENTLY JOINED A POLITICAL ORGANIZATION.

My decision to join politics created quite a furore. Although a large section of my friends and admirers appreciated and welcomed it, there were many who were not happy. They either expressed their displeasure through personal messages or wrote it on my social media pages. They felt that I had already created my identity and had established myself as a well-known

Giving Back to the Society

hairdresser and hence there was no need to join any political establishment.

Some were also of the opinion that by becoming a primary member of this political organization I would lose my credibility. They also felt that getting affiliated to a particular set-up would mean that I would become

Jawed Habib with Delhi BJP Chief, Manoj Tiwari

unacceptable to a large section of the Indian society. There were many more apprehensions, but I know that they were candid in expressing their fears because they were my well-wishers. The question asked by all was: Why did I join a political organization?

To answer this question, I will explain what I want in life. What is the motto of my business? What do I want to do? How do I wish to be remembered? These are extremely important aspects of a human being's life. These are the factors that shape a man's life. These are the things that should be clear in everybody's mind. Because once these ideas are clear in your mind, you will know precisely what you wish to do in your life. You will create your own path. You will not have to depend on destiny or, maybe, you will not need an excuse like 'I was not destined' to get it or do it in life.

Most of us think and behave as if destiny is preordained, and so we just sit back and do nothing. A few, however, believe that they have the capacity to change, and so they act accordingly. I belong to this group. I believe that I have the power to make my own destiny with my thoughts and actions. I genuinely believe in myself that I have the power to do things according to my way. For me, destiny is the result of actions you perform with a positive frame of mind. My destiny follows the purpose that I have set for my life. My life and my actions have not been pre-decided by any unknown and intangible concept called destiny. I am the master of myself. My instincts and hard work push my destiny to help me reach my goals.

NOBODY GETS TO WRITE YOUR DESTINY BUT YOU. YOUR FUTURE IS IN YOUR HANDS.
—BARACK OBAMA

WHY CAN'T A HAIRDRESSER BE A POLITICIAN?

When entrepreneurs, bankers and lawyers can be politicians, then why can't a hairdresser be one? I want to send this message to everyone in this country that you don't need to have a certain background to get into politics. All you need to have is determination and the zeal to serve.

As you all know, I was not born with a silver spoon in my mouth. My grandfather was a simpleton, a barber working as a Class IV staff of Rashtrapati Bhavan. My father too started his career in that manner. We lived in a humble quarter. My father was hardworking and enterprising enough to go out of India (to London) to take a course in hairdressing and subsequently opened his own store in New Delhi. I was born on the premises of Rashtrapati Bhavan, and I had spent my initial years there. From this seemingly privileged but not truly-so beginning, I have grown to become one of India's most successful hairdressers. It was a long and arduous journey. I had to hear unsolicited comments like *'o taa sirf aek nai hai'* (he is just a barber) or *'uske pitaji toh sirf ek nai hai'* (his father is just a barber). All these words used to pinch me. Today, no one dares to make such annoying comments, but still I know that there are many who believe that I am just a glorified *nai*. I have no qualms about it, but what I dislike is the negative undertone of such comments. Despite my and my family's success, this has remained with me.

A GENUINE LEADER IS NOT A SEARCHER FOR CONSENSUS BUT A MOULDER OF CONSENSUS.
—MARTIN LUTHER KING, JR.

Why do we look down upon the profession of hairdressing? I find it very disturbing to see that hairdressing, as well as several other jobs that truly benefit the society, are looked down upon. I have seen many people, usually well educated and sometimes extremely successful in their own professions, who act in a condescending manner towards people who do such jobs. Any work that primarily involves manual labour or something done by a pair of hands as opposed to working with the 'head' is generally looked down upon. Unfortunately, people perceive that barbers do not use their brains; they only work with their hands. I find such behaviour obnoxious and unacceptable. However, finding a good barber is like finding a good lawyer or a good doctor, and a person goes back to him/her again and again.

A NAKED TRUTH: THE MORE YOU EARN MONEY, THE MORE YOU EARN RESPECT IN SOCIETY.

Your work is never considered a parameter of measuring your success. It is only your earnings that matter. If I put it in a different manner, it will be such that if you are not economically well off, then you, as a person, and your views will not be accepted in the society. Thus, the natural propensity is that a person's income is the sole, accurate and the most proper indicator of that person's value and the contribution that he/she makes to the lives of others. So, the source of societal respect is actually the money that you earn. Is it the way a capitalist society behaves? I am not too sure, but one thing is certain and that is I do not like it and believe it.

EDUCATION IS THE NEW ROUTE

Throughout my life, I have been telling everybody that I have the power to change this profession and this change will come only through education.

EDUCATION IS THE MOST POWERFUL WEAPON WITH WHICH YOU CAN CHANGE THE WORLD.
—NELSON MANDELA

There is no alternative to education and there are no shortcuts either. It is only education that will change the paradigm of this profession. A haircut will remain the skill of a hairdresser's fingers and hands. That will not change, but there will be several differences between a trained and skilled hairdresser and an unskilled or untrained one. For any and every job, competence is the prerequisite to succeed. Competence comes from experience and education. An educated hairdresser will have the power to go a long way. He/she will understand a client's needs properly. He/she will be able to communicate with clients in a better manner and with confidence. He/she will be able to adapt to future changes. He/she will be empowered to bring changes.

CATALYST TO THE CHANGE

The motto of my life is to provide education to all the hairdressers of this country and bring noticeable and substantial changes in their lives for their betterment. Like me, they should also earn respect from society. I want to be the catalyst to this change. And to achieve it, I will have to reach out to all of them. I know it is easier said than done.

Have we ever calculated how many hairdressers are in this country? This question has come up in my mind several times. I have a simple answer. I do not know whether the social scientists and the economists or the experts in social studies will accept it. At present, the population of India is around 130 crores. Even at a conservative estimate if there is one hairdresser for every 100 Indians, then there should be 1.30 crore hairdressers. It is a huge number. It is almost the size of the total population of Jammu and Kashmir.

I have said that I organize and attend seminars and workshops on hairdressing. On average, I hold 50 such workshops in a year, which is roughly four a month. So, even by a conservative estimate, if say 150 hairdressers attend a workshop, it means I actually meet approximately 600 new hairdressers ever month or about 7,500 of them every year. So, over the past 25 years, I have managed to meet about 1,87,500—about 2 lakh hairdressers. Now, I can add to it the number of students who undertake hairdressing courses in my Jawed Habib Hair Academies. In the 64 training centres we have, if 25 students pass out in a year, that is, approximately two every month, then this means that 1,600 students graduate every year. Over the past 10 years, a maximum of 16,000 have passed out. Hence, despite all my efforts and network, I have been able to touch upon only around 2 lakh dressers, which is only 1.5 per cent of the 1.30 crore hairdressers of this nation.

Critics may point out that there are several other organizations which are also imparting hair education. I do not disagree with them. The National Skill Development Mission, which was launched by the Union Ministry of Skill Development and Entrepreneurship on 15 July 2015, also works on this skill. The National Skill Development Corporation, a non-profit public limited company established in July 2008, is doing a great job too. I am also associated with these activities of the government. In fact, the curriculum for hairdressers and beauticians used by the National Skill Development Corporation is prepared by me and my organization. Several state governments are also working on this front on their own.

We are working with several of these governments even outside the purview of the National Skill Development Mission.

Apart from this, we have worked with the Central Reserve Police Force and the Punjab Police for training a section of their personnel in hairdressing. Interestingly, we have also trained convicts in the Agra Central Jail. These inmates now run a salon within that campus. We are also working with His Holiness the Dalai Lama in Himachal Pradesh for training hairdressers.

There are many private-sector organizations, both corporates and educational institutions, who also impart training in hair education. Although none of them has the network or the tenacity like me, still if I accept that there is a confluence of all others' efforts along with mine, then also the total number of educated hairdressers will only double to around 4 lakhs from 2 lakhs, which is again only 3 per cent of the total number. The rest 97 per cent, which is 1.26 crore, is still deprived of getting a proper hair education. There is a universe in front of me.

Now, the question is: How can I reach these hairdressers? That is the challenge! According to the last census carried out in India in 2011, there are 497 cities, 7,935 towns and 6,49,481 villages. The census also said that around 68 per cent of the Indian population lived in 6.5 lakh villages. And as the father of our nation, Mahatma Gandhi said, 'The soul of India lives in its villages', I will have to take my education to the hairdressers who are living in these villages as well.

To do that, I need the support and patronage of a political establishment—a national party that has a reach beyond our imagination. They are present in the maximum number of Indian cities, towns and villages. To take my education beyond the level I have reached, I will have to leverage this network. I will have to convince the *nai*s (the barbers) of this country that they will have to educate themselves to become trained hairdressers. By education, I mean vocational training, proper grooming in hygiene and exposure to new methods, techniques and technologies. Few will be opposed to it too. The community for whom I wish to take this education will oppose as none wishes to change. I know most of them are happy with what they are doing and the way they are doing it. It is either a lack of ambition or the level of comfort in what they have. They will not like to come out of their cocoon. Therefore, I need the support of a political establishment. Acceptability of a local but a true political leader, who really believes in bettering the lives of the people, is extremely high. He/she can be a member of a gram panchayat or a councillor in a municipality. Their support is necessary. Would we have witnessed a Green Revolution in India without political support or for that matter the White Revolution? Who knows that we may soon witness a Hair Revolution?

If I succeed in convincing the leaders of the political establishment of what I wish to do, then I am sure that they will help me in getting connected with the masses. Yes, I need the support of a political party, but it is not for my personal gain or for the expansion of my corporate network. I already have a team of dedicated professionals and passionate partners who have been and will continue to work on it. And on top of it, I have my zealous hairdressers. They will propel the growth of my business enterprise. However, for reaching out to all my fellow hairdressers and to help them change the way they are working, my sole efforts will not be enough. A push and guidance from the political establishment are extremely necessary.

I was going through the reactions and the comments that were made on my social media pages immediately after I joined the political organization. Some were extremely harsh and unfair, some were outright nonsense and there were some who tried to mean that a representative of an enterprise joins a political establishment only for his/her organization's gain. The most common and ideal notion is that when you become a politician, you are supposed to look after the interests and well-being of the common man/woman of the nation. If we believe that a doctor or a lawyer or a singer or a film star will rise above his or her personal interests and work for the masses, then why do we doubt the integrity of an entrepreneur? I think that this is wrong and this mindset has to change. Entrepreneurs and businessmen are also citizens of this country. If a social worker dreams of doing something good for the underprivileged section of society, so can a businessman. My fellow citizens of this country should mature and stop dividing society with such a parochial outlook. I am aware of the social commitments and social work being done by several business magnates of this country at a personal level beyond the requirements of their corporation's corporate social responsibility. They do not do it for the attention of the media. They do not want any publicity. They do it because they feel that it is their duty to give it back to the society they belong. I would like to appeal to those who see a financial gain behind everybody's activities that there is a heart in every human being which does not always follow what the head says. Entrepreneurs and businessmen are human beings too and they also belong to this Indian society. People should respect when they try to bring some social changes beyond the purview of their corporations' gains; at times, people become petty and too personal when they look into the bigger picture. I think these efforts should be appreciated and welcomed.

Now, why does a large section of our society hate politicians? I know many of you will say the following. Most of the politicians are involved in corruption. Public money is looted through scams, and the poor sections of the society are deprived of their basic needs and requirements. Another opinion is that politicians think that they are the supreme authority in their constituencies. They feel that they are beyond the laws of the land. If not them, at least, their followers act in that manner. Most feel that politicians are mean and self-centred. They only look after their personal gains. Although their apparent objective is to serve the masses, still most think that it is just a mask and behind it, they only fulfil their personal interests. These views of the masses are universal and not just restricted to India.

POLITICS MEANS SERVING THE NATION

Politics is about corruption, that's how most people view it. I do not subscribe to this view. Neither are all politicians corrupt nor are they all busy boosting their personal gains. If that had been so, India would not have improved on the social, financial and economic parameters in the last seven decades.

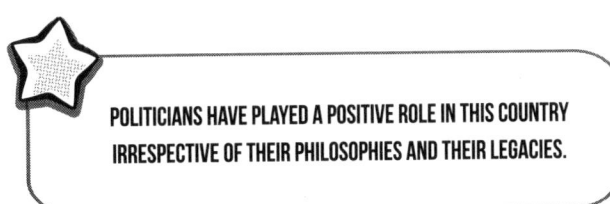

POLITICIANS HAVE PLAYED A POSITIVE ROLE IN THIS COUNTRY IRRESPECTIVE OF THEIR PHILOSOPHIES AND THEIR LEGACIES.

I also do not disagree with the fact that we have witnessed rampant corruption amongst them. I don't think that we should be making sweeping generalizations. Everyone should be individually judged on the merit of their work. I also feel that if I wish to change the way political establishments work, I will have to be a part of it. It is easy to stay away and criticize, but it requires a certain amount of boldness to enter that arena and change it.

> I AM A DOER, AND I HAVE ENTERED POLITICS TO ACT.

I am a doer, and I will do good work. For me, it is spreading the education on hair and improving the lives of my fellow hairdressers, no matter where they are located in this vast country of ours.

ACCESSING SMALL AND REMOTE VILLAGES

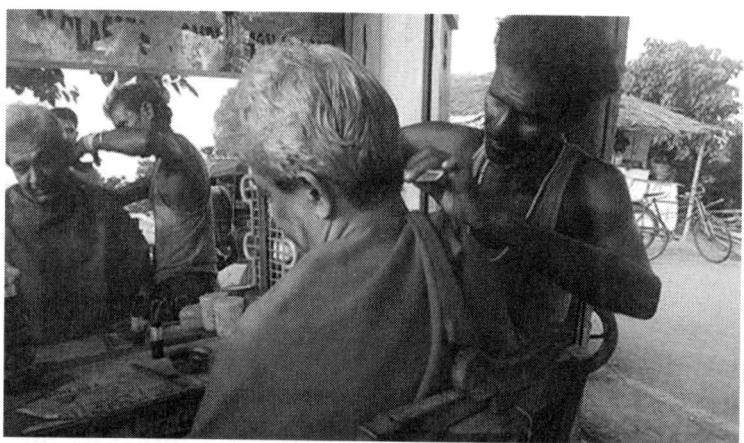

Talented Indian Barbers

We can add an introductory line—'Knowledge and awareness do play a major role in the modernization of any place.' However, the sad part is that our villages haven't been able to see this light because somewhere entrepreneurs haven't been capable enough in reaching out to them. Although I travel by road in India to some nondescript locations or to a small and little-known town, I make it a point to visit the local saloons or the barber shops there. I meet the hairdressers there and talk to them. I ask about their livings. I look at the equipment they use. I have even taken haircuts from them. Many of them recognize me and hesitate to open up, but after some time they get comfortable with me and tell me their stories. I have uploaded videos of several such interactions on my YouTube channel. I do all this to be a part of the lives of these people. After all, they are my colleagues. We are in the same profession. I have seen that there is tremendous scope for improving their lives and I wish to contribute to it. I hope that my decision of joining a political establishment will help me achieve it.

MY JOURNEY AND MY LEARNINGS

CHAPTER TEN

SUCCESS IS NOT FINAL, FAILURE IS NOT FATAL: IT IS THE COURAGE TO CONTINUE THAT COUNTS.

WINSTON CHURCHILL

The journey of human life is a journey through the lanes and by-lanes of failures and successes. No one has achieved success in life without groping through the darkness of failure. Success always comes with a lot of pomp and show. Success gives you a push—an impetus to drive you on this journey of life. It makes you a hero and masks your shortcomings and weaknesses. We do not analyse our success; we usually celebrate it. Since childhood, society teaches us how to manage success, but failures are never discussed. We are never taught how to overcome failures. We cope with failure in our own ways.

FAILURE IS NOT AN ANTONYM OF SUCCESS. IT IS A SYNONYM OF LEARNING.

Failures are like the unknown pitfalls on a road. You never know when you will fall. With failure, you can either lead yourself to despair or you can turn yourself around to success. It is natural to feel low and lose interest when things do not go the way they have been planned. You should use failure to reassess yourself and reset the perspectives and priorities in your life. Failure is necessary to shake things up. Without it, one will just sail around and will not look for the shores. It makes you stronger and improves your ability to take on bigger and more difficult challenges in life. It is the primary ingredient of success. It keeps a check on your confidence and balances your ego. When every deal is cracked and business is on a rise, failure helps you to remain grounded. It makes you humble and prepares you for the uncertainties of the future.

I was also prepared for the future by some instances that I encountered in my life.

On 31 January 2011, I decided to go for an initial public offering (IPO). We filed for a ₹60 crore IPO and spent 10 per cent of this amount initially. We were supposed to get approval, but someone made a complaint against us.

This didn't happen once, but twice. As a result, I decided to withdraw my application.

We had spent ₹6 crores on marketing and suffered a total loss of around ₹18–20 crores.

This could have been thought of as failure for most people, but I didn't take it as one. I was part of the press all this time since I was the first hairdresser of India to file for an IPO which made headlines everywhere. It was also a sort of marketing for my brand, and I would like to thank god because my business increased 3–4 times after this incident.

For people, ₹20 crores is a loss, but for me, it was the amount that got channelized into the marketing for my brand.

The setbacks in your life should not stop you from winning in future. When we come across the name 'Einstein', we generally associate it with intelligence and scientific knowledge. This also means genius to many. However, it is a well-known fact that this famous German-born physicist, who is known for his theory of relativity, could not speak fluently until the age of 9. His rebellious nature led to expulsion from school, and he was refused admission to the Zurich Polytechnic School. His setbacks in his early life did not stop him from winning the Nobel Prize in Physics for his explanation of the photoelectric effect in 1921. He could achieve this, because he believed, 'success is a failure in progress'.

The 16th President of the United States of America, Abraham Lincoln, badly failed in his business in 1831. He also suffered a nervous breakdown in 1836. He was defeated in his run for Presidency in 1856. Rejection and failure were a part of his life. Instead of getting bogged down, he kept on striving. 'My great concern is not whether you have failed but whether you are confident with your failure', he had said. According to him, the amount of rejection one receives in life is not the defining factor because 'success is still within your reach'. Lincoln was elected as President in 1861 and he remained in that position till he was assassinated in April 1865.

Steven Spielberg is a household name all over the world. He is considered as one of the most influential filmmakers that the world has ever seen. However, what many do not know is that the director of *Jaws, E.T. the Extra-Terrestrial, Jurassic Park, Indiana Jones, Schindler's List* and many other famous films was rejected by the University of Southern California, not once but thrice. While he was in college, he was noticed by the representative of Universal Studios and he was signed as a television director in the year 1969. This meant that he could not finish his college for many years. He was eventually awarded an honorary degree from the same university in 1994, and in 1996 he became a trustee of that university. In 2002, 35 years after starting his college career, Spielberg finished his degree. He received his B.A. in Film Production and Electronic Arts with an option in Film and Video Production. After all, perseverance and acceptance of failure are the keys to success. Bad grades in high school failed to dampen the spirits of this great filmmaker. 'Even though I get older, what I do never gets old and that is what I think keeps me hungry', he had said.

J.K. Rowling, the author and the creator of *Harry Potter*, at a commencement speech in Harvard cited the importance of failure. According to her, she was the biggest failure of all:

> I had failed on an epic scale. An exceptionally short-lived marriage had imploded, and I was jobless, a lone parent, and as poor as it is possible to be in modern Britain, without being homeless. The fears that my parents had for me, and that I had for myself, had both come to pass, and by every usual standard, I was the biggest failure I knew.

However, she overcame everything and emerged a stronger and determined human being. That is the contribution of failure in our lives.

The second incident that I encountered was in Malaysia. It was my company's first step out of India. I bought a salon brand called Clipso International. This happened in the year 2008, before the IPO incident. I invested ₹1 crore—considered a big sum at that time—in this company which had two hair academies in a central area of Kuala Lumpur.

But it was an overpriced investment. The consultant and the team that we had roped in for this purpose had not done their homework well. It proved to be a completely wrong decision and a bad investment. As a result, we moved out of that market. Again, I would not consider it a failure, but a learning, as this prompted me to make many other wise decisions.

I have had my own share of failures in my personal life too. But these failures have not curbed my *junoon* (passion). My passion has remained with me despite my failures. Some call it craziness, but I love my craziness. My madness has helped me stay focused on my work. I have not wavered from the two mottos of my life: to educate the hairdressers of this country and to give a haircut to each and every citizen of this country.

> I THINK THIS CRAZINESS OF MINE IS EXTREMELY POWERFUL. IT HAS WORKED WONDERS FOR ME AND ONE DAY IT WILL TAKE ME TO THE WORLD THAT I DREAM OF.

This passion for hair service has made me work in some of the weirdest places one can think of. Just because of this passion, I keep scouting for opportunities all the time and everywhere. Giving a haircut comes naturally to me. I do not care where I am or to whom I am giving a haircut. Location is also not a factor at all. You will be surprised to know that I have done a haircut in a house, at a railway station, at an airport, in the flight, on a train and even on the street. I just need a pair of scissors. I have worked with kitchen scissors and first-aid scissors. On a lighter note, I can say that I can give a haircut even with a pair of gardening scissors if the situation demands.

I am not finicky about cutting sheets, styling chairs or combs. On several occasions, I have used the newspaper as a cutting sheet. Any chair can be a styling chair for me. And the magic spell is cast, literally empty-handed. Hairstyling is my passion and I have made my passion my profession.

I WANT TO CONTINUE BEING CRAZY; LIVING MY LIFE THE WAY I DREAM IT, AND NOT THE WAY THE OTHER PEOPLE WANT IT TO BE.
—PAULO COELHO

Passion is the love that makes a professional successful. Without passion, one's profession is just a job to earn a livelihood. It will not make him/her great. Virat Kohli has succeeded as a cricketer because he enjoys playing cricket. The world would not have seen the greatness of Lionel Messi or Cristiano Ronaldo if they had not enjoyed playing soccer. All those who have achieved greatness in life have succeeded in doing so because they did what they loved doing the most. They did not wait to hear what others are saying about them. They carried on and on despite their successes and failures.

Yes, failures in life are as true as the successes you achieve. But if one has passion and zeal, he or she will come out of failures. These are roadblocks on the journey to greatness; you just need to swirl past it. When you are driving a car, you do not stop seeing a bumper. You just drive over it. Treat the failures of your life as those insignificant hindrances. At most, these are speed breakers. They do not have the power to stop the car, as the steering wheel is still in your hands and the accelerator beneath your foot. So, just drive over your failures. Do not look back, but take your lessons along.

Failures in my life revolve around some of the business decisions that I took but did not work. Like a true entrepreneur, I depend on my instincts. I am more of an instinctive businessman rather than being research-oriented. I love to follow my gut feelings. I do not wait to take actions, because I feel that a delayed decision is mostly a wrong decision. The crucial factor is time, and you miss out on it. Yes, I have made mistakes.

My decision to acquire a Malaysian brand did not work the way I wanted. My dream of getting my company listed on the bourses has not happened yet. But in both cases, I took it in my stride.

Maybe I was ahead of time, maybe the time was not right or maybe things would have been different if we had gone ahead with some other consultant. With regard to our application for the IPO, now I feel that I was ahead of time. Many people failed to understand the core strength and functioning of Jawed Habib Hair & Beauty Ltd and our business model at that time. However, I neither repent nor look back. These two experiences of mine have helped me learn several things. Today, I am more knowledgeable and I know how to succeed in overseas markets. While there were these failures, there were these moments of achievement when I represented Sunsilk as their brand ambassador. For a hairdresser to become a brand ambassador is certainly a matter of achievement.

Jawed Habib Was the Brand Ambassador of Sunsilk from 2000 to 2008

I have also pondered on why a plan fails. Generally, it is said that a plan fails either because of poor planning or poor execution. In other words, it means that either the strategy was not right or the way it was implemented was incorrect. As I said, as a person I generally do not introspect, but here I have learnt my lessons. So, I know what went wrong and I am confident that it will not happen in future. I had my quota of learning from those occurrences.

Along with failures, another thing that I have always ignored in my life is criticism. Like Bob Dylan, I would like to tell my critics, 'Don't criticize what you do not understand.' There is no need to avoid criticism because if one tries to avoid it, then he will be forced to say nothing, do nothing and be nothing in this world.

> AS WE SHOULD NOT LET ARROGANCE DEFEAT OUR SOUL OR DESPAIR KILL OUR HEART AND COMPLIMENTS GO TO OUR HEAD, THE SAME WAY, WE SHOULD NOT ALLOW CRITICISM TO BEAT OUR EFFORTS.

Several near and dear ones of mine have first criticized me and my business plans. Then when they saw me succeed, they started following me silently.

They never understood what I am planning and why I am planning or what my plans are. Most of them have not agreed to my ideas, forget supporting me. However, when I found them copying my concepts and following my business practices, it gave me a sense of achievement. It made me feel accomplished.

I have always believed that whatever you do in your life, good or bad, there will always be some people who have something to say against you. They will criticize, but I know that the person who is criticizing does not have the ability to achieve what I have achieved. My simple approach to criticism is to ignore because when someone is trying to bring me down, it only means that I am higher than him or her. Ignoring them does not mean that I have not taken note of them. It only means that they are really not important and that they are not worth my time. Somewhere I had read, critics are like parrots, they talk much, but dreamers are like eagles, they say nothing but rule the skies. Also, there is another section of critics who criticize me because so many people appreciate me.

Let me talk about my venture in Bangladesh, our dearest neighbour. I have been trying to do something in that country for the past 15 years. I had partnerships with many. Unfortunately, most of it has not worked. Despite starting on a good note, things went wrong. Either the partners have not realized my dream and did not understand my working style or they felt that they were prominent as compared to me in their market. Whatever might be the reason, the result was not what I wished for. They thought that they had introduced me to that market. But I realized that I had no control over what they thought. So, I allowed them to keep on thinking whatever they felt. I only knew what I wanted to do. So I did what I am best at doing. I just kept on trying and trying. You will be surprised to know that I have done hairdressing seminars not just in Dhaka but even in Chittagong, Pabna and Jessore. My efforts have borne fruits. Today, I can happily say that I have partners who believe in my dreams, who know what I want and who are equally confident and positive like me. My vision is only focused on my goals.

Another instance of my learning was in London. I was in love with London as I had attained my education there. It was the start of my professional success. I opened a salon in Southall in London which was in operation for almost three years. But somehow it didn't work much in our favour, and after three years, we decided to hand it over to a buyer in London.

But this didn't dissuade me from not trying again. I persisted and opened a new salon in 2006 in London. I took my trained staff from here and got work permits for them. Those eight people chose to leave me for better opportunities one by one which forced me to shut down the business in London. However, after a few years, I started an education centre in London.

Article in the *Hairdressers Journal International*

I always felt that London was a good market and I had the potential to do well there. I still visit London to see what else I can do.

This brings me to another interesting aspect. So many people think that Jawed Habib has become Jawed Habib because of them, as they had either organized my seminar in that city or opened my first salon in that region. This group of people tend to take all the credit. For them, just organizing a workshop or starting a salon was the only recipe for my success. I wonder how easily they have forgotten my years of hard work, determination and dedication. Have they forgotten how hard I have worked with my students and clients? Have they forgotten my hours and hours of teaching or my patience in hearing my clients and giving them quality service? Success has many friends and everyone would like to take credit for your success.

I am sure that they also know it, but they are too narrow-minded to accept it. This brings me to another aspect of my life, to the people around me. I am never short of admirers and followers. I have experienced the love of my followers. A lot of people are encouraged by my success and want to emulate it and that makes me happy. I share my dreams with them. I also share my business ideas with them. I give people the opportunity to work with me. Some of them like it and join hands with me. Most of these people have stayed with me, but I have lost others. The journey of life is like that.

I don't hold any grudges. Although I remember the ones who have helped me and done well for me, I don't like to mull over or hold grudges against people who have cheated me. I only believe that every person has a particular role to play for a limited period of time. Beyond it, they become insignificant. I have never disrespected their contribution or disregarded their involvement. All of them have left a positive impact on me. I have only forgotten the bitter part of my journey as I have moved on with my life and my dreams. I do not waste time contemplating on things like 'what would have happened if he was with me' or 'he should not have felt that way' or 'he did not understand what I meant'. These are negative approaches and they have no space in my mind.

I keep on sharing this analogy with my friends, partners and employees. My life is like a running train. It started from one station and only I know when my terminal station will come. Many have boarded it and have alighted too but my train has kept on moving. From 1 salon to 900 salons, 1 academy to 65 academies, 1 city to 121 cities, 1 state to 24 states and 1 country to 4 countries. It will not stop. I am moving on. I request my partners to be a part of my success story. I will not stop. I do not know how to stop.

My journey is like that famous song 'The Strange Case Of ....' by the rock band Halestorm.

Head lights, red lights, got it in my sights
Nothings in my way, No sound, hush now
Push the pedal down, got no time to waste
It's a long way home, You just crossed a borderline
When I say go, You know you better hold on tight
I don't know how to stop, I give it all I've got
It's like my brakes are shot, I gotta have too much
I don't know how to stop, Gets crazy but so what
You know it's what you want so give it up
And Don't be scared of how good it feels

One speed, full speed that is all I need
They can eat my dust, hell yeah, rock on
Will you come along, Do I have your trust?
It's a long way down, If you're getting this high
When I say now, you had better hold on tight
Now! ....

I don't know how to stop
I don't know how to stop
I don't know how to stop

Life for me is not a destination. It is a journey and my work is my vehicle. I do not aim to earn more money or get more fame. I love my work and I love doing it every day. No amount of failure will be able to stop me. I just move on in life. Several years back, I heard the following Sanskrit *sloka* and it left a deep impact on my mind.

Charan vai madhu vindati, Charan swadum udumbaram
Suryasya pasya shremanam, Yo na tandrayate charan
Charaiveti, Charaiveti

Loosely translated, as someone explained to me, it means that the honey bee, by its movement, collects honey and birds enjoy tasty fruits by constant movement too. The sun is revered and respected because of its constant shining movement. Therefore, one should be constantly in motion. Keep moving, keep moving on.

I am not a Vedic scholar, but these words have always fascinated me. Later on, I learnt that Gautam Buddha used to chant the words 'Charaiveti, charaiveti' after his sermons every day. It simply means to move on and be a dogged traveller in the journey of life through the highs and lows, crests and troughs, tides and ebbs, failures and successes. I have nothing left in yesterday, but I have tomorrow to gain everything.

I am a simple and common man. I take lessons from my daily life. So, I believe that every day is the day I am getting married. So, I wake up my liveliest best. My eyes are shining in hope. I am most cordial with everyone. I have the widest smile on my face. I believe this attitude of mine sets me up for success day after day. After all, attitude is everything!

ABOUT THE AUTHOR

A name synonymous with hairstyling and fashion care in India, Jawed Habib is the Chairman of a leading hair and beauty chain Jawed Habib Hair and Beauty Ltd.

Considered as one of the top hairstylists in the industry, Jawed Habib is known for his association with film and fashion celebrities. Jawed entered his name in the *Limca Book of Records* by giving a whopping 410 haircuts in a day. Jawed has also been the brand ambassador of the famous hair care product brand, *Sunsilk*, and has also been the official hairstylist for Femina Miss India, 2003.

Jawed joined the Bharatiya Janata Party in April 2019. Jawed believes that education can add value to any profession and has a chain of academies where young hairstylists are trained and moulded every day. Not only are they taught the intricacies of hairstyling, but they are also trained in providing excellent service experience to the customers.

Coming from the prominent family of the hair and beauty business where his grandfather Nazir Ahmed was the official barber for Lord Mountbatten and

Jawaharlal Nehru, Jawed believes that learning is a never-ending process. He attributes success in this profession largely to education.

Jawed completed his studies in French Literature from Delhi University and pursued specialization in Hair Design from The Morris School, London.

Rohit Prasad's wonderful book, *Game Sutra: Rescuing Game Theory from the Game Theorists,* is a collection of dozens of real-life applications of game theory. Written in English—that is, without mathematics—it is accessible to the educated general public. Entertaining, informative and fresh, it is strongly recommended to anyone who is interested in discovering how human interaction works.

Noble Laureate Robert J. Aumann
Economic Sciences, 2005

Your guide to understanding game theory

For special offers on this and other books from SAGE, write to marketing@sagepub.in

Explore our range at
www.sagepub.in

PAPERBACK
9789353285722

> The authors' basic belief in the subject of values and their core intent of helping others comes through as they articulate the concepts and also provide some structured mechanism for introspection and development of a value system for oneself ... this book is a facilitator for anyone who wishes to seriously reinforce a culture of values in the organization.
>
> **S. Viswanathan**
> Chief People Officer, NIIT Technologies Ltd

Values in business

For special offers on this and other books from SAGE, write to marketing@sagepub.in

Explore our range at www.sagepub.in

PAPERBACK
9789353284558

> *Seeing Digital* is an exceptionally well-done piece of work. It combines both an in-depth macro-economic analysis of the impact of the digital age, with all of its micro implementation challenges, while containing a number of useful frameworks to help parse the future. Not a comfortable read, but a very important one.
>
> **F. Warren McFarlan**
> *Professor, Harvard Business School*

Creating a transformational digital world

For special offers on this and other books from SAGE, write to marketing@sagepub.in

Explore our range at
www.sagepub.in

PAPERBACK
9789353286392